DATE DUE

DEMCO, INC. 38-2931

Scrapbooking Just for You!

Scrapbooking Just for You!

How to Make Fun, Personal, Save-Them-Forever Keepsakes

by Candice Ransom

STERLING

New York / London

STERLING and the distinctive Sterling logo are registered trademarks of Sterling Publishing Co., Inc.

Library of Congress Cataloging-in-Publication Data

Ransom, Candice F., 1952–
  Scrapbooking just for you! : how to make fun, personal, save-them-forever keepsakes / Candice Ransom.
     p. cm.
  Includes index.
  ISBN 978-1-4027-4096-1 (alk. paper)
  1. Photograph albums—Juvenile literature. 2. Photographs—Conservation and restoration—Juvenile literature.
3. Scrapbooking—
Juvenile literature. I. Title.
  TR501.R37 2010
  745.593—dc22

2008038982

Lot #: 10 9 8 7 6 5 4 3 2 1
12/09

Published by Sterling Publishing Co., Inc.
387 Park Avenue South, New York, NY 10016
© 2010 by Candice Ransom
Distributed in Canada by Sterling Publishing
^{c}/o Canadian Manda Group, 165 Dufferin Street
Toronto, Ontario, Canada M6K 3H6
Distributed in the United Kingdom by GMC Distribution Services
Castle Place, 166 High Street, Lewes, East Sussex, England BN7 1XU
Distributed in Australia by Capricorn Link (Australia) Pty. Ltd.
P.O. Box 704, Windsor, NSW 2756, Australia

Printed in China

Sterling ISBN 978-1-4027-4096-1

For information about custom editions, special sales, premium and corporate purchases, please contact Sterling Special Sales Department at 800-805-5489 or specialsales@sterlingpublishing.com.

Design and layout by *tabula rasa* graphic design
Photography by Robert Malmberg and Dan Wonderly

DEDICATION
To the members of "The Island":
Connie, Sioux, Pamela and Terri.
And to LaJune Lundquist.
Without your friendship and
encouragement over the years,
I would never have
attempted this book.

contents

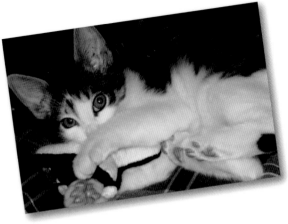

The Secret in the Spare Room

In my grandparents' house, the door to one room was always closed. Once, when I was nine years old, I slipped inside and discovered the secret in the spare bedroom.

The room held a four-poster bed, a bureau, and a vanity with a blue leather hassock. I lifted the button-tufted lid of the hassock and found a book with a black cover.

I opened the book across my lap and saw that it was a photo album whose solid black pages had been turned so often, they felt like cloth. Paper corners anchored the black-and-white photographs.

I didn't know any of the people in the pictures. Who was that baby in a high chair? Who were those two boys holding the baby goats?

Whenever I visited my grandparents, I also visited the photo album. Each time I opened the black cover, the pictures told me new stories.

Around that time, I began creating things from paper. Diamond shapes snipped from notebook paper and glued to crossed twigs became tiny kites. Shoeboxes were turned into haunted houses. I made teeny greeting cards for my stuffed animals.

Later, I found a store that sells scrapbooking papers and supplies. I noticed scrapbookers—people who make scrapbooks—gathered at the back of the store, and, fascinated, I joined them and began an album of my own. I made mistakes—lots of mistakes—but I kept working and learning.

When I cut paper and mat photographs, I am telling stories. As I learned more and tried new techniques, I discovered a secret, like the photo album I'd found years before: Scrapbooking makes me feel good!

Now you, too, can create memory books that tell the story of your life. And here's one more secret—scrapbooking is fun!

Getting Started

A Short History of Scrapbooking—How It All Began

So, what is a scrapbook? Basically, it's a book in which mementos and photographs are preserved.

The first scrapbooks, dating back to the fourteenth century, were called commonplace books. People copied poetry, proverbs, quotes, and other written material into bound books. President Thomas Jefferson pasted leaves, poems, letters, and quotes into his books. Mark Twain, author of *Adventures of Huckleberry Finn* and *The Adventures of Tom Sawyer*, spent Sundays working on his collection. Victorian-era girls kept friendship albums, in which they preserved ribbons, dried flowers, and poems from their friends.

Where did the word "scrapbook" come from? In the nineteenth century, blank books were sold to paste in letters and newspaper articles. These were called scrapbooks. Women snipped pretty pictures from calendars, cigar box labels, and valentines and pasted them in their scrapbooks. This hobby became so popular that printers decided to create and sell pictures already cut out and ready for pasting. These images were called "scraps." Designs ranged from angels to birds to high-button shoes, and they sold like crazy!

When George Eastman invented the Kodak camera in 1888, anyone could take photographs with his simple camera. People began pasting photographs in their scrapbooks.

Keeping a scrapbook was a popular pastime in the first half of the twentieth century. Girls filled their books with photographs, movie ticket stubs, drinking-straw wrappers, four-leaf clovers, lucky pennies—anything they wanted to save forever.

Today, making scrapbooks is one of the most popular hobbies ever. There are entire stores that sell nothing but scrapbook supplies, albums, and craft paper. Craft stores hold classes in special techniques such as stamping and paper folding.

You are about to enter the exciting world of scrapbooking. Let's get started!

How to Use This Book

This book is divided into three main sections. This first section gives you basic information. The next section is all about page layouts. The third section is filled with ideas for gifts, journals, and other projects that lead to the "Grand Finale" scrapbook party. In the back of this book you'll find a glossary of scrapbooking terms.

Read through the first section. Next, practice working with your tools and supplies. Then begin your scrapbook album or, if you like, go straight to a project in section three.

Today's scrapbooks consist of three parts: photos; patterned papers, stamps, stickers, and other supplies; and words. Though you'll see some wordless layouts and projects in this book, try to include journaling in yours. Pictures tell only half the story.

3

By adding your thoughts and memories, you'll make your scrapbook projects a lot more fun to look back on in the future.

Throughout the book, I have used stickers, alphabet stamps, and rub-on transfers to create titles, words, and phrases. You can try any of these techniques, or type the words out on your computer, or print them by hand.

The layouts in chapter 6 are presented with the simplest techniques first; each technique may be shown in several different examples that also demonstrate other techniques. All the techniques described are presented from easiest to most challenging. At the bottom of each project, you'll find a list of supplies used. This list contains all or most of the materials used and their manufacturers. If you want to duplicate the project, the supply list will guide you. But remember, this is an *idea* book. Use different colors. Experiment with sticker placement. Substitute different papers, trims, and embellishments to reflect your personal style and taste. After all, these projects are all about *you*!

Stuff You Might Be Wondering About

Card stock and paper come in 12" × 12" and 8½" × 11" sizes. Why are the layouts in this book smaller?
12" × 12" is big—really big. It's hard to fill that space and still have nice-looking pages. 8½" × 11" is an odd size. Pages work better when they are a perfect square. The projects in this book are ideas. You may prefer making bigger or even smaller pages.

None of the layouts in this book use more than a few photographs. Why? I have lots of pictures!
Good! You'll be able to make lots of albums and other projects. Check out my "bad" layout on page 14. You'll see that too many photographs on one layout look messy and random. Scrapbooking isn't about gluing a ton of pictures on a page. It's about highlighting a few special photographs and telling the stories behind them.

I don't live near a special store that carries scrapbook supplies. Where can I buy card stock, paper, and tools?
Craft stores such as Michaels, Hobby Lobby, and A.C. Moore all have well-stocked scrapbooking departments. You'll see projects in this book that use items from office supply stores, sewing stores, and even hardware stores. You'll also see layouts that use basic card stock and little else. If you really want to shop at a scrapbook supplies store, your parents may be willing to help you shop for supplies online—there are hundreds of scrapbook supply Web sites out there.

How do I find the exact papers that are used in these layouts?
The projects in this book are here just to spark ideas for you to create your own personal pages. Feel free to change the colors of the card stock, the patterns of the paper, and other details. But if you really do want all the products used in these layouts, the supplies and their manufacturers are listed at the end of each project.

Can I use stationery and wrapping paper in my layouts?
Stationery is fine, but avoid using wrapping paper, which is too thin and will tear.

What is cropping? It sounds like something a farmer would do!
Cropping is a scrapbooking term for trimming and cutting. You *crop* a photograph to get rid of the parts that aren't interesting. A *crop* can also be a party, where you gather with your friends and work on your scrapbooks.

Why are none of the pictures in the layouts in the middle of the page? Everything is on one side or the other.
The elements in a scrapbook actually look better off center. The eye prefers objects in odd numbers, at interesting angles, or off center. If you place your photos smack-dab in the middle of the page, you'll have trouble fitting the title, journaling block, and embellishments.

All the photographs in this book have a colored border around them. Do I have to do that to my pictures?
The colored border is called a photo mat, and it's made from card stock. You can highlight a color from the photograph with a mat, and I think mats make photos look more "finished." But if you like adhering your pictures "naked" on the page, that's okay, too!

Can I put other stuff besides photographs in my scrapbooks?

You bet! Feel free to add mementos—movie tickets, e-mails, fortune cookie fortunes—anything that you want

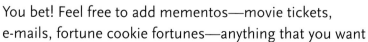

to keep belongs in your scrapbook. You can also include pictures and blogs downloaded from the Internet or CDs, and magazine articles and pictures.

My page doesn't look perfect like the one in the book. Help!
Scrapbooking isn't about being perfect. Most pages, even those created by professionals, have mistakes that only *they* can see. Scrapbooking is about making pages that please you.

A Short List of Don'ts

- ☺ Don't use construction paper instead of card stock—it's too flimsy.
- ☺ Don't write on your photos with anything but a permanent marker—pencils leave marks and ballpoint pens smear.
- ☺ Don't trim or cut Polaroid photographs—they leak chemicals.
- ☺ Don't use Scotch tape, masking tape, rubber cement, or school glue—they aren't safe for your papers or photos. Use special glues and tapes just for scrapbooking.
- ☺ Don't crop original photos—*always* use copies.

Basic Supplies and Tools

How Much to Buy?

As you would with most new hobbies, expect to buy tools that you will use more than once, such as a trimmer, scissors, and hole punches.

You will also need to buy consumables. These are products that are used up, such as paper, card stock, embellishments, and adhesives. Watch your newspaper for sales at your local craft store. Stock up on adhesives and card stock to save money.

Acid-Free Paper and Supplies

When you buy scrapbook supplies, you will often see the words "acid-free" on the label. Acid destroys photos. Fortunately, nearly all scrapbook products—

papers, card stock, glues, stickers—are photo-safe. But don't worry if you want to use a magazine picture in your layout, and don't feel you have to use purchased products in your projects.

Where to Store All the STUFF?

Scrapbooking supplies have a way of taking over the world! A few inexpensive containers will corral your tools and supplies.

- ☺ A large file folder box, found in an office supply store, is perfect for storing card stock, patterned paper, and sheets of stickers. Make sure the box is big enough to hold 12" × 12" paper.
- ☺ Old muffin tins are great hold-alls for rubber stamps. You won't have to worry about the bottom of the tin getting smudged with ink.
- ☺ Use empty baby food jars or other small jars with lids to store buttons, beads, charms, brads, and other small embellishments. Ribbon scraps are easier to see in larger jars.
- ☺ If you don't have a special place to work on your scrapbook projects, keep your tools in a plastic carryall made for cleaning products. When you're ready to work, grab your carryall, file box, and latest project, and spread out on the kitchen table.

Card Stock

The stiff paper called card stock forms the base for your pages. You will also mat photos with card stock and use it to make tags, journaling blocks, and other details for your layout. Card stock comes in every shade imaginable, so you can mix and match colors.

Patterned Paper

Walk into any scrapbook store, or down the scrapbook aisle of your craft store, and you'll see dozens of papers printed with designs. The type of patterned paper you use will set the tone for your page. In this book you'll learn to mix patterns to give your pages zing.

Albums

Scrapbook albums come in all sizes and colors. They are also constructed with different kinds of bindings.

- **Post-bound** is the most common type; the album and pages are bound together with screws and posts.
- **Strap-hinge** albums are bound with plastic straps threaded through staples on card stock pages.
- **Three-ring** albums are similar to school binders; pages in these albums can be rearranged easily.
- **Spiral** albums have metal or plastic coils to bind heavy card stock pages

Albums are found in different sizes: 12" × 12", 8½" × 11", 8" × 8", 6" × 6", and even smaller. You'll need an 8" × 8" album for the projects in this book.

When choosing your album, think about your personal style. Do you follow trends? Flip over anything pink? Let your album tell the world who you are.

Plastic Page Protectors

Post-bound, strap-hinge, and some three-ring albums come with plastic page protectors. These plastic sleeves open at the top or on the side. Slide layouts inside to keep them from getting dirty or torn.

Stickers and Rub-on Transfers

Everyone loves stickers! Craft and stationery stores have entire aisles stocked with hundreds of different stickers. Alphabet stickers, animal stickers, flower stickers, stickers with glitter—the list goes on. Stickers add interest to your pages and let you be creative. Plus they are fun to collect!

Similar to decals, rub-on transfers are burnished or rubbed onto paper with a Popsicle stick or a burnishing tool. Rub-ons are terrific! You can add words and designs to paper, card stock, even photos. They come in a huge variety of alphabet designs and images. I like rub-ons better than stickers because the edges are "invisible."

12" Paper Trimmer

Paper trimmers cut clean, straight edges with a very tiny blade that is protected by the blade holder. You'll use a trimmer for cutting patterned paper and card stock and for cropping photos. Trimmers have grids and rulers that help you cut the correct size. The swing arm beneath the base extends the ruler to 15".

You'll use this tool for every project. Although there are several styles to choose from, all trimmers have a small blade that runs along a track, grid marks, and a swing-arm ruler.

Scissors

You'll need a good pair of detail scissors. Look for scissors that have sharp edges and pointed tips. Small finger holes with rubber grips are the most comfortable. Always store them with the protective cap over the point, and never use the scissors to cut anything other than paper or card stock.

Decorative-Edge Scissors

Available at every basic craft store, these cool scissors cut edges in a variety of styles.

The trickiest part of using these fun scissors is continuing a cut. Pay attention to the design pattern and fit the blade into the next groove or scallop to avoid "choppy" cuts. Don't use these scissors to crop photos; they will tear the edges of photo paper.

See-through Ruler

A clear plastic ruler will allow you to draw straight lines and measure photos, layouts, and mats. A plastic see-through ruler will lie flat on your projects, and you'll be able to see photographs and your layout while measuring.

Adhesives

The adhesive aisle in the craft store contains a dizzying array of glues. For the projects in this book, you will need a glue stick, liquid glue, and glue dots. Double-sided sticky tape that comes in a dispenser is optional for mounting photographs.

Adhesive Devices

These nifty devices turn clip art, punches, small photos, and alphabet letters into stickers. The adhesive cartridge comes in permanent or repositionable (meaning that you can move the sticker before deciding where you want to place it permanently). Insert your image into the slot and pull the strip from the other end. Remove the sticker from the adhesive strip.

Rubber Stamps and Ink Pads

You can create many different looks with one or two rubber stamps and a pigment-based ink pad. Decorative stamps are a fun alternative to stickers and can be used over and over. Stamped images can be colored with pens and colored pencils. Sets of alphabet stamps are a great way to create page titles.

Instead of pressing the stamp block into the ink pad, run the ink pad along the stamp to apply ink over the whole design. When stamping paper, do not rock the stamp. (Rocking the wood block will blur the image.) Press downward with even pressure to avoid stray ink marks.

Pigment Pens, Gel Markers, and Colored Pencils

You may already have a bunch of these fun pens! Pigment ink is waterproof and won't fade. You'll need a black fine-tipped pen for journaling. Add gel markers in rainbow shades, glitter pens, puffy 3-D pens, and metallic pens to round out your collection. Use colored pencils to add color to stamped images.

Alphabet and Shape Templates

Templates are a snap to use. Lay the template over your photograph or paper and trace lightly with a pencil. Cut out the shape with detail scissors.

Punches

A punch is a handheld tool that punches out squares, circles, hearts, flowers, and other shapes. You'll need a circle punch (1½" diameter), a corner rounder, and a one-hole punch (the kind you squeeze in your hand for notebook paper). In this book, punches in square, flower, and heart shapes are also used. To make sure your paper is within the circumference of the punch, check the bottom before punching.

Photographs—Let's Get Snapping!

I am the world's worst photographer. In my pictures, people's heads are cut off. Buildings are crooked. Dogs always have their eyes closed. So I'm not the person to give you lessons on how to take better pictures. But I *can* help you organize, choose, and crop your photos.

Digital Photographs

Most of us own digital cameras. These cameras are great because you can instantly see if you've taken a good shot. You can also download pictures to a computer and store them, using a photo editing program. These programs allow you to darken, lighten, reduce, enlarge, and crop your photos before printing. Some photo-editing programs, such as Picasa and Photoscape, are free. Most discount stores offer photo printing services or kiosks where you can print your own photos.

Photography has become much simpler with the invention of digital cameras. But any point-and-shoot camera—even a disposable camera—will do. Polaroid cameras are fun to have at parties, for instant pictures.

Storing Photographs

Are all your pictures in a big box under your bed? Or still in the paper folders from the film-processing store? Are your class field-trip pictures jumbled with photos from last year's vacation?

- Get all your pictures out of the box or paper envelopes. Sort them into piles: by year, by event (holiday, vacation, etc.), or by people (friends, relatives, etc.).
- Using a 4" × 6" file box, place each group of photos behind a tabbed index divider.
- Write the name of the category on the divider. Every time you have pictures developed, place them behind the proper index divider.

Selecting Photographs

If you have 16 photographs from cheerleading camp, how do you decide which ones to put in your album? You could use all 16 in a special album. But if you are making a page for your school-year album, for example, you would want only two or three. Choose photographs that show action, people, or close-ups of interesting objects.

Cropping Photographs

Even bad pictures can be salvaged. Simply cut away distracting portions, such as doorways or windows, and focus on the interesting parts.

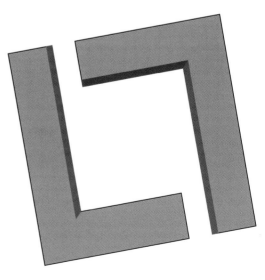

If you have trouble deciding what should stay and what should be cut, make a set of L bars. Buy a precut photo mat from a framing or craft store. Cut through two of the corners to form two Ls. Alternatively, you can make two Ls from cardboard.

Use the L Bars Like a Window

- ◐ Move the L bars around on top of your photo, creating a frame around different areas of the picture, to see what parts are worth saving.
- ◐ Mark the photo lightly with a pencil, all four sides, showing where you want to crop.

- ◐ Trim the photograph with your paper trimmer.
- ◐ Don't forget you can also crop on your computer.

Silhouette Cropping

By cutting a photo around a figure or a head, rather than with a straight line, you create a silhouette. Silhouettes add interest to your pages.

Matting Photographs the Easy Way

While you can glue your photos directly to the background or patterned paper, they look better with a mat.

1. Choose a sheet of card stock that brings out one color in the photograph.
2. Place your photograph on the card stock so that one corner of the photo fits into one corner of the card stock.
3. Ease your photo down and sideways until the border is the width you want it to be; eyeballing about ¼" all the way around is good. Mark the two sides of the card stock that need to be trimmed.
4. Adhere your photograph to the card stock. Tape runners work best and can be applied before you position the photograph.
5. With your trimmer, slice off the remaining two sides of the card stock. With practice, you'll be able to judge the space between the edge of your photograph and the track on your trimmer without marking.
6. Your photograph is matted and ready to adhere to the page!

tip

Journaling blocks also look better matted. You can even mat stickers to keep them from becoming "lost" on the page.

Layouts

Designing Your First Layout

What Are Layouts?

Layouts are the pages that go into your album. The most basic layout contains:

- A background, usually card stock
- Photographs
- A title
- A caption or journaling block

But you'll see you can go way beyond basic! Your layouts can be simple—or they can be filled with glitz and glitter.

How Do You Make a Layout?

This book will give you lots of ideas. Layouts are designed so that the photographs, paper, and embellishments look pleasing. Sample layouts are presented in this book with the simplest techniques demonstrated first; subsequent techniques are more challenging. Each technique may be shown in several different examples that also use other techniques.

You will want to take a look again at the "Basic Supplies and Tools" section in "Getting Started." Specific things you will need are listed for each layout, but some tools are used for almost every layout and aren't always listed each time:

- Paper trimmer
- Scissors
- Adhesives (glue, glue dots, glue stick)
- Permanent black pen
- Pencil
- Ruler

Don't Let the Word DESIGN Scare You

Creating each page involves selecting, cropping, and arranging photos. You'll learn step-by-step how to mat photos, use patterned papers, and add embellishments—stickers, buttons, and so on. You'll learn how to make pairs of pages—called double-page spreads—work in your albums.

Turn the page to see what a layout should *not* look like.

"Bad" Layout—Don't Let This Happen to You!

Okay, you might wonder, "What's so bad about these pages?" At first glance, they don't seem awful. Look at the pages again and think about the following questions:

- ☺ Does the white background do anything for the photographs?
- ☺ Are the captions clear and easy to read?
- ☺ Which picture grabs your attention?
- ☺ When you look at the pages, where do your eyes travel? Left to right? In a circle? All over the place?
- ☺ Do the pictures appear to "float" on the pages?
- ☺ Do the stickers have anything to do with the photographs?
- ☺ What are these two pages about? Why kind of story do they tell?

Let's discuss this layout point by point:

- ☺ **White background:** The pictures appear "lost" on the white card stock. Color adds punch to your pages and makes photographs pop!
- ☺ **Captions:** Handwritten captions are fine, but the corrected misspelling looks sloppy. Two of the captions are about events, three are comments, and the stuffed-elephant photo doesn't even have a caption. You should tie all of the photos together with captions about the event or the people.
- ☺ **Focal point:** None of the photos grabs your attention because they all compete with one another. No single picture seems more important than the others.

- ☺ **Composition:** No, this isn't about an English essay, but about how the pictures are arranged. The photographs in this layout are spread over both pages in such a way that your eyes flit from top to bottom and side to side.
- ☺ **Anchor:** "Anchor" is another word we'll use a different way. Photographs need to be anchored, or grounded, on the page. The pictures on these layouts aren't positioned in relation to anything else on the page. Even the stickers are floating.
- ☺ **Sticker sneeze:** Don't grab a tissue! A "sticker sneeze" is what happens when you scatter stickers on the page like confetti. School stickers, craft stickers, and the sheriff's badge sticker don't make sense together.
- ☺ **Story:** These two pages don't tell us anything. We don't know why these particular pictures are grouped together. The Thanksgiving photo has nothing to do with the bratty brother photo or the pony. The layout has no overall theme.

So How Do You Make Good Layouts?

Easy! By following a few simple rules of design, you'll create pages that tell a story, please the eye, and show off your artistic side. And you won't come down with a "sticker sneeze" attack!

Thanksgiving at Grandma's

Mom! Ha-Ha!

Bratty Brother!

Mom! Look at that hair!

Chincoteague Pony Ride

15

Designing Your Page—The Rule of Three

Just as in fairy tales, three is a magic number in design. Three elements or items—a photograph, a title, and some sort of embellishment—are all you need to make your first page!

I chose the Pony Ride photo from the "bad" layout. It has action and a pony!

Because the photograph is somewhat dark, I used pink card stock for the page background. to bring out the pink shirt. Next, I matted the photo in a darker shade of pink to make the page pop. The photograph is Element #1.

I like big alphabet stickers, but a whole title made up of them won't fit on one page. So I used the capital "P" and "R" with smaller alphabet stickers to spell out the title. Whoa! Small and large alphabet stickers—isn't that two items? Not really. Because the title is in a block, it forms one unit. The title is Element #2.

The blue sheriff's badge sticker didn't do much for this photo on the "bad" layout. But the cowgirl in red and tan is just the ticket. The sticker is Element #3.

What's So Magic about Three?

Three elements on a page form a visual triangle. A visual triangle is a path your eyes follow. The path leads to the main element: the photograph. And three items look pleasing on a page.

Notice that I added a strip of the darker pink card stock to anchor the cowgirl sticker, so it doesn't "float" on the page. I could have printed my caption on the strip, though I chose to write under the photo. Either way is fine.

Supplies Used: Card stock, Bazzill Basics; stickers, Close to My Heart

Element #1
The Photograph

Element #2
The Title

Element #3
The Sticker

Pony Ride

My aunt riding a Chincoteague Pony!

Using Color—Does Color Matter?

When you get dressed in the morning, do you sometimes ask yourself, "Do these colors look okay together?" You don't usually want to wear colors that clash. So, yes, color matters.

You may be familiar with a color wheel—a circle with pie-shaped segments of color—but you may not know how it works. Here's a crash lesson.

Colors Are Divided into Three Main Groups

- **Primary colors** are the "pure" colors of red, blue, and yellow.
- **Secondary colors** are formed by mixing two primary colors to create orange, green, and violet.
- **Tertiary colors** are formed by mixing two or more secondary colors to make red-orange, yellow-orange, yellow-green, blue-green, blue-violet, and red-violet.

All of these colors can be found on a color wheel. Let's put it to work. Have you ever thought about why red and green look great with each other? Or why autumn colors like yellow-orange, orange, and red-orange seem just right together? It's largely because of where these colors fall on the color wheel.

- **Neighboring colors:** Also called *analogous*, colors that are next to each other on the color wheel go together. For example, look at the colors on either side of orange—yellow-orange and red-orange. There are your fall colors!
- **Opposite colors:** Also called *complementary*, these colors are directly opposite each other on the color wheel. Opposite red is green. They work because they contrast each other.
- **One color, many shades:** Also called *monochromatic*, these colors vary in lightness or darkness. You could use different shades of pink on your layout, from light pink to medium pink to dark pink.

You may be wondering, "Do I always have to use the color wheel? Can't I just pick my favorite colors?" Absolutely! Your scrapbook should show the world who you are. If you love all things purple, then go for it!

But if you want variety in your layouts, or if you are stumped about what color card stock to pair with a certain pattern of paper, the color wheel will help you. It's a tool, just like your scissors and paper trimmer.

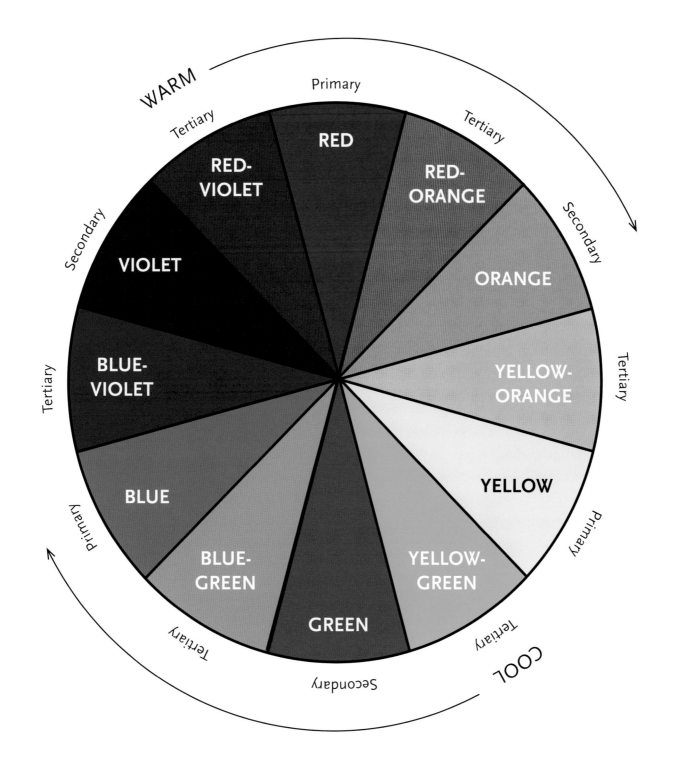

19

Layout: "Emily"

Hello! My name is Emily. I dug this great big hole because it seemed like a good idea. First I dug a little, then I dug more and more. I couldn't stop! Now I wish I had a glass of iced tea. And I wish a big wave would wash the sand off me. But first . . . will somebody help me get out?

EMILY

waves

water

Ocean City MD

bubbles

Decorative-edge scissors create really cool borders. But you can also use them to create a special effect, such as clouds, sky, or water.

To make the "Emily" layout, you'll need decorative-edge scissors with a wavy or wide scallop pattern.

1. Cut the medium blue card stock to create two 8" × 8" pages.
2. Trim your photo, and mat it on dark blue card stock.
3. Cut a 7¾" × 7¾" piece of the beach paper, and adhere it to one piece of the medium blue 8" × 8" card stock.
4. Adhere the photo to the page, placing it 1½" from the left and 1¼" from the top so the photo is off center.
5. Cut an 8" × 2¼" strip of the dark blue card stock, and trim it with wavy scissors.
6. Cut an 8" × 2½" strip of the light blue card stock, and trim it with wavy scissors.
7. Cut an 8" × 3" strip of the white card stock, and trim it with wavy scissors.
8. Adhere the dark blue piece to the light blue piece, and the light blue piece to the white piece.
9. Adhere the wave strip to the bottom of the second medium blue 8" × 8" card stock page.
10. Write or type your journaling in a square, mat it with scrap of beach paper, and adhere it above the "waves."
11. Add a title or titles at the bottom of the page.
12. Add flowers and other stickers, overlapping them onto the photo, the photo mat, and the journaling mat for interest.
13. Apply glitter glue to highlight the "waves" and accent the flowers. Be sure to let glitter glue dry overnight.

Supplies Used: Card stock, Bazzill Basics; patterned paper, Me and My Big Ideas; stickers, KI and Anna Griffin; glitter glue, Ranger

You Will Need

2 sheets of medium blue card stock
1 sheet of dark blue card stock
1 sheet of light blue card stock
1 sheet of white card stock
1 sheet of summer- or beach-themed paper
Stickers
Glitter glue
Wavy scissors

tip

For your journaling square, write more than just the facts. For example, the picture tells us only that there is a girl sitting in a sandy hole. Journaling tells us why she dug the hole, how she dug the hole, and the fact that she can't get out. Write as though you are talking to the person looking at the photograph.

Layout: "Gypsy Witch"

I was a gypsy fortune teller at the school carnival. I waved my hands over a crystal ball. But I couldn't think of any fortunes! Whenever I talked, I giggled! Finally I said to a boy, "You will take a trip." He said, "Yeah, I'm going to the baseball dunking booth." We both laughed. It was so funny!

Purple and red—do those colors get along? Yes, they do, especially if they are joined with red-violet, the neighboring color between red and violet on the color wheel.

Use any three neighboring colors on the color wheel without worry. Yellow, yellow-orange, and orange would make a sizzling summer layout. Green, yellow-green, and blue-green are the colors of spring.

In the "Gypsy Witch" layout, red, red-violet, and violet look great together. Since there is light purple in the photograph, a red mat makes the purple pop. Purple is repeated in the card stock strip mounted on the red-violet page.

I created the accents by color photocopying and reducing the images from a book, then running them through a Xyron sticker maker. Three red self-adhesive "jewels" echo the jewels in the photograph.

1. Cut the sheet of card stock to create an 8" × 8" page.
2. Cut one piece of card stock in a neighboring color into an 8" × 3½" strip.
3. Crop and mat the photo on a third color of card stock, and adhere it to the page.
4. Apply three stick-on jewels in a row below the photo.
5. Write or type a journaling block, mat it, and adhere it to the page.

Supplies Used: Card stock, Bazzill Basics; stick-on jewels, My Mind's Eye, Design Originals

You Will Need
1 sheet of card stock
Card stock scraps in "neighboring" colors
Stick-on jewels

tip

Try creating your journaling on the computer using the colors in your layout.

Layout: "Dog Birthday"

If you have a really great photograph, you may not want to "lose" it in busy patterned paper. Instead, show off that special photo by creating a monochromatic color scheme for it.

With card stock and a few stickers, you can create a colorful page that lets the photograph shine.

Monochromatic color schemes are easy. Select a color and add two shades of the same color. The "Dog Birthday" layout uses shades of purple (from darkest hue to lightest: grape, violet, and light orchid), taking its cues from the paper plate in the photo.

The medium shade, violet, forms the page backgrounds. The darker and lighter shades, grape and light orchid, can be used as borders and as mats for some of the stickers. The photograph is matted in bright green to highlight the green icing and napkin design.

Create easy borders with inset pieces of card stock, and try strip journaling, one of the hottest trends in scrapbooking: type up your journaling block, leaving plenty of space between the sentences. Print, and cut into strips.

Today is Duncan's birthday! He's five years old!

He could go to kindergarten. Do they have dog kindergarten?

Duncan loved his cake. He got icing all over his nose!

I gave him a new chewie toy. He tried to bury it!

Then he went to sleep. I guess parties make him tired.

1. Cut the medium card stock to create two 8" × 8" pages.

2. Cut one piece of light card stock so it measures 8" × 3". Create a border by adhering it ½" from the left side of one of the 8" × 8" pages.

3. Mat the title sticker on dark card stock. Trim so the mat matches the shape of the sticker, and adhere it to the border. This keeps the sticker from becoming "lost" on the side with the lighter card stock border.

4. Crop and mat the photo. Adhere it to the page, overlapping the border.

5. Cut a piece of light card stock to measure 8" × 4". Adhere it to the second 8" × 8" page, flush with the right side.

6. Cut a piece of dark card stock so it measures 8" × 3". Adhere it over the light border, ½" from the right edge.

7. Cut your journaling into strips. Adhere the strips to the page.

8. Mat a large sticker on dark card stock. Trim the mat so it matches the shape of the sticker, and adhere it to the page.

9. Apply stickers.

Supplies Used: Card stock, Bazzill Basics; stickers, K & Company

Layout: "Dance"

With some photographs, you don't want to use busy patterned paper or brightly colored card stock. It's time to head into neutral territory. You can't go wrong with a neutral hue, such as black, paired with a brighter color.

Black and pink make a classic combination. Add a little white, and you have a layout that's as pretty as your first dance dress. Here, black photo mats look striking against the pink background. A black-and-white polka-dot border runs down the side of one page and across the other.

A few stick-on jewels, a simple caption in glitter stickers, and a dramatic flower are all the embellishments this layout needs.

You Will Need

2 sheets of pink card stock

1 sheet of black card stock

1 sheet of black-and-
white polka-dot paper

Stick-on jewels

Rub-on transfers (optional)

Glitter alphabet stickers

Silk flowers

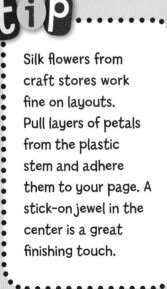

tip

Silk flowers from craft stores work fine on layouts. Pull layers of petals from the plastic stem and adhere them to your page. A stick-on jewel in the center is a great finishing touch.

1. Cut the pink card stock to create two 8" × 8" pages.

2. Crop and mat the photos with black card stock.

3. Cut the polka-dot paper into two 8" × 2" strips.

4. Adhere one polka-dot strip across the first 8" × 8" page. Adhere the smaller photo 1¼" from the right edge and 1" from the bottom edge of the page.

5. Mat your journaling block. Adhere it in the upper left corner, overlapping the photo. Apply three stick-on jewels vertically on the journaling block.

6. Write or use rub-on transfers to spell "glamour girl" or a phrase of your own in the bottom left corner.

7. Apply glitter alphabet stickers to the upper right-hand space, overlapping the first one with the journaling block.

8. Adhere the larger photo to the second page, 1" from the right edge and 1" from the bottom edge.

9. Adhere the second polka-dot strip vertically, ½" from the left edge of the page.

10. Using glue dots, apply silk flowers to the bottom right corner of the photo.

Supplies Used: Card stock, Bazzill Basics; stick-on jewels, patterned paper, Heidi Swapp; rub-on, Me and My Big Ideas; alphabet stickers, Provo Craft; flowers, Doodlebug

DANCE

My first dance.
I love my dress
and my necklace.
And my shoes!
All my friends
will be there.
Will anybody ask
me to dance?
My first dance.

glamour girl

tip

For instant poetry, write a phrase like "My first dance," describe your feelings about that phrase, and end by repeating the phrase.

Layout: "Making Dad's Cake"

To keep the focus on your photo, create a visual triangle. If you place your embellishments in three spots around your photo, people will see the picture first. Cropping is also important. In the photo for the "Making Dad's Cake" layout, the background was cluttered with chairs, windows, things on the table, and other people. Try to crop your photos closely to the center of the action. Use your L bars, if necessary (see page 10).

The "Making Dad's Cake" layout is simple, consisting of patterned paper and scraps cut into circles. Pen "bubbles" are added to continue the line of the visual triangle.

1. Cut the patterned paper to create an 8" × 8" page.
2. Mat your photo with the scrap of card stock.
3. Punch out circles of different sizes from the scraps of patterned paper.
4. Position your matted photo on the page, but don't adhere it yet.
5. Arrange your circles so a large group is near the lower left corner of the photo, a smaller group is near the upper left corner, and a third group is near the bottom right corner.
6. Lightly adhere your matted photo to the page. Slip a large circle under the top left corner of your matted photo and adhere it to the page.
7. Continue adding circles in each of the three groups. Let some circles overlap one another and overlap the photograph.
8. With your pen, outline the circles and the photo mat to add definition. Draw "bubbles" from the lower left corner of the photo to connect the two groups of circles on the left.
9. Let more "bubbles" trail upward from the circle group on the right.
10. Write your journaling beneath the photo. Add the date inside one of the bubbles if you wish.

You Will Need
1 piece of patterned paper
Scrap of card stock
Scraps of patterned paper
Circle punches

Supplies: Card stock, Bazzill Basics; patterned paper, Bo Bunny, Junkitz, and Scenic Route; pen, Sakura.

tip

If you don't have circle punches, cut circles by hand. Turn your paper instead of your scissors for smoother rounded edges.

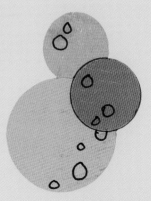

Layout: "Feelin' Feline"

CAT NAP

My cats are so funny!
Winchester sleeps on his back
with his feet sticking up in the air.
Persnickety likes to have her tummy
rubbed. Sometimes she gets mad
and scratches but she's just playing.

feelin'
FELINE

queen of sheba

Your shoebox is overflowing with pictures. How do you sort them and begin making layouts? One way is to look for common features.

Let's say you have a gazillion pictures of your dog. In one picture he's wearing a bandanna, in another he's sleeping, and in a third he's catching a Frisbee.

Instead of making a page of different doggy poses, put the Frisbee-catching snapshots together for a dynamite layout. You can write about how he's "doggedly" after someone to play Frisbee with him.

In my own shoebox of pictures, I found I had more photos of our cats stretched out than in any other pose. I combined two of the cutest in a one-page layout.

1. Cut one sheet of card stock to create an 8" × 8" page.
2. Crop and mat the photos using the contrasting-color card stock.
3. Adhere the matted photos to the page, overlapping corners.
4. Apply stickers and rub-on transfer.
5. Print or type a journaling block, and adhere it to the page.

Supplies Used: Card stock, Bazzill Basics; stickers, Stickopotamus; rub-on transfer, Bo Bunny

tip

Rub-ons can be used on paper, chipboard, metal, wood—even photographs.

You Will Need
1 sheet of card stock
1 sheet of card stock in a contrasting color
Stickers
Rub-on transfer

Layout: "Petey the Parakeet"

Four Things a Parakeet Shouldn't Do
by
Petey

1. Perch on a human's head. My feet got tangled in her hair!
2. Ditto. *What* is this slick stuff in his hair?
3. Don't get too close to humans when they are giggling. I nearly fell off!
4. Don't let humans act up. This guy is *sooo* embarrassing.

If you have a bunch of so-so pictures that have the same or similar subjects, you can make several of them look great by keeping them together on a single page.

In this one-page layout, four 4" × 6" photographs have been cropped to 2" × 3¼". At 2" wide, these four pictures fit perfectly across an 8" page.

With this many photographs, patterned paper may look too busy or even become distracting. This easy layout uses only card stock and simple sewing trims.

1. Cut one sheet of card stock to create an 8" × 8" page.
2. Crop photos to 2" wide and 3¼" long.
3. Cut the contrasting-color sheet of card stock into a mat measuring 8" × 3¾".
4. Adhere the photographs to the mat, edge to edge, as shown.
5. Adhere the matted photos to the page, 1" from the bottom.
6. Type or print your journaling block on a scrap of white card stock.
7. Mat the journaling block with a third shade of card stock, and adhere it above the photos.
8. Cut a 4" length of ribbon, fold it into a V, and adhere it near the journaling block.
9. With a glue dot, adhere the button over the point of the ribbon V.
10. Glue the rickrack along the bottom of the page.

Supplies Used: Card stock, Bazzill Basics; ribbon, rickrack, Making Memories; button, Doodlebug

tip

Write from the pet's point of view! What would an animal think about humans? Pet pictures are often humorous, so try to make your journaling funny, too!

Layout: "Play Mousie"

Although scrapbook and craft stores are filled with hundreds of different patterned papers, you may want to add your own personal touch. This is easily done by jazzing up black-and-white patterned paper with markers or colored pencils. Keep your page from being overwhelmed by choosing only two colors.

Look for patterned papers that have areas you can color, such as large flowers or leaves. Don't forget about the spaces between images. To make this layout truly your own, add a hand-cut title embellishment.

1. Cut the patterned paper to create an 8" × 8" page.

2. Crop and double mat your photo with two pieces of contrasting-color card stock.

3. Position your matted photo on the layout, and lightly outline it in pencil.

4. With markers, color parts of the design on the black-and-white patterned paper. Keep the focus on your photo by creating a visual triangle. Color one section above, one below, and one to the side of your photo.

5. Adhere your photo, covering some of your colored design.

6. To make the mouse embellishment, draw on scraps of card stock an oval with pointed ends, as shown. Draw an eye and nose and pen stitch (draw small, sketchy little lines that imitate the look of sewn stitches) around the body. Punch two ears from card stock.

7. Adhere the mouse to your layout. Adhere the ears, sliding one beneath the head.

8. If you want a tail, cut a length of black embroidery thread. Tuck it under the mouse's body before adhesive is completely dry.

9. Write the title on the mouse.

Supplies Used: Patterned paper, Luxe Designs; markers, Sharpie; pen, Sakura

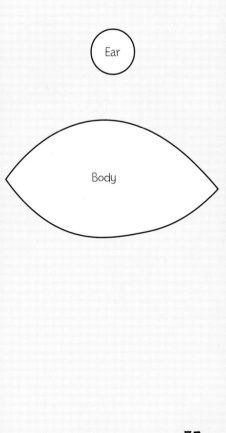

You Will Need
1 sheet of black-and-white patterned paper
Markers or colored pencils
Scraps of card stock
Small round punch
Black embroidery thread (optional)

Mouse Pattern

Ear

Body

Layout: "I Am . . . Me!"

Some pictures don't need a lot of journaling. Or maybe you don't have room for a journaling block on your layout. Why not let word stickers and rub-on transfers do the work?

Stickers and rub-on transfers come in tons of words, phrases, and type styles. Domed stickers add variety and interest. Try covering a boring spot on your photograph with a rub-on. In the "I Am . . . Me!" layout shown here, the flower rub-on brightens the blank corner and picks up the background color.

Don't forget punctuation. Alphabet sticker sheets often come with punctuation marks. Combine "orphaned" stickers—asterisks, exclamation marks, and parentheses—with word stickers for a fun layout that describes you to a T!

1. Cut the two sheets of card stock to create two 8" × 8" pages.
2. Crop and mat the photos in contrasting-color card stock.
3. Adhere a photo to one page of the card stock.
4. Apply title stickers.
5. Apply punctuation stickers, domed stickers, and rub-on transfers.
6. Add a rub-on word or design in one corner of the photograph.
7. Cut the patterned paper into a 7¾" × 7¾" square. Adhere it to the second card stock page.
8. Adhere a photo to the second card stock page.
9. Continue the title in the lower right-hand corner of the second page.
10. Apply dome stickers, word stickers, and rub-on transfers.

You Will Need
2 sheets of card stock in the same color
1 sheet or scraps of card stock in a contrasting color
1 sheet of patterned paper
Domed word stickers
Word and punctuation stickers
Word rub-on transfers

Supplies Used: Card stock, Bazzill Basics; patterned paper, Sassafras Lass; domed stickers, Making Memories and Me and My Big Ideas; rub-on transfers, Me and My Big Ideas and Junkitz; alphabet stickers, Reminisce

goofy

cute

fun

Layout: "A Friend for Life"

Here's an easy way to fill your journaling block—make a list! You can make lists about anything: "My Ten Favorite Songs," "Five Reasons Why I Love Soccer," "Eight Funny Things My Dog Does." You can even split your list into two categories: "Five Things I Love About School" and "Five Things I Don't Like About School."

Study your photograph and brainstorm possible lists. Once you figure out the subject, write down ideas as they come to you. Type your list on the computer or print it by hand.

You can create an entire mini-album with your list. Each page can be a different numbered point.

1. Cut the two sheets of card stock into two 8" × 8" pages.
2. Crop and mat your photo with the contrasting-color card stock.
3. Cut the patterned paper into a 7¾" × 7¾" square and adhere it to the first page.

You Will Need
2 sheets of card stock in the same color
1 sheet of card stock in a contrasting color
1 sheet of patterned paper
Stickers
Chipboard heart

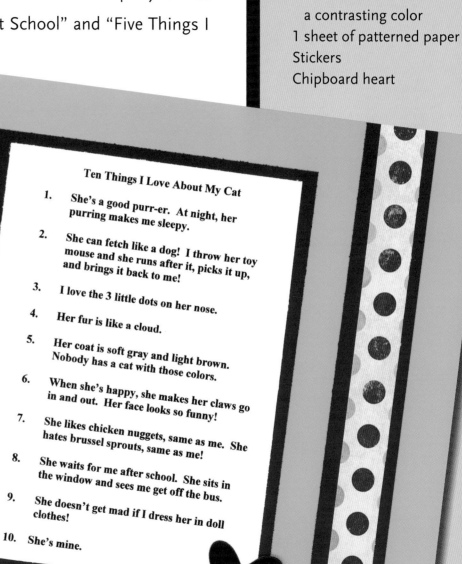

Ten Things I Love About My Cat

1. She's a good purr-er. At night, her purring makes me sleepy.
2. She can fetch like a dog! I throw her toy mouse and she runs after it, picks it up, and brings it back to me!
3. I love the 3 little dots on her nose.
4. Her fur is like a cloud.
5. Her coat is soft gray and light brown. Nobody has a cat with those colors.
6. When she's happy, she makes her claws go in and out. Her face looks so funny!
7. She likes chicken nuggets, same as me. She hates brussel sprouts, same as me!
8. She waits for me after school. She sits in the window and sees me get off the bus.
9. She doesn't get mad if I dress her in doll clothes!
10. She's mine.

4. Adhere the photo to the page, and add stickers.

5. Mat your journaling block on contrasting-color card stock.

6. Adhere your journaling block to the second page, positioning it to the left.

7. Cut an 8" × 1¼" strip of contrasting-color card stock. Adhere it down the right side of the page.

8. Cut an 8" × ¾" strip of patterned paper. Adhere it down the center of the border.

9. Adhere the chipboard heart.

Supplies Used: Card stock, Bazzill Basics;
patterned paper, stickers, Bo Bunny; chipboard heart, Heidi Swapp

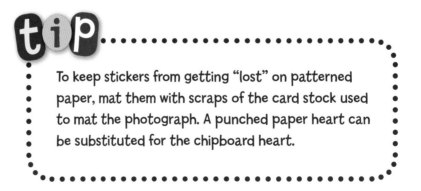

tip

To keep stickers from getting "lost" on patterned paper, mat them with scraps of the card stock used to mat the photograph. A punched paper heart can be substituted for the chipboard heart.

Layout: "School Project"

Computer journaling is fast and easy. It's also versatile. You can change font styles, sizes, and colors (if you have a color printer).

If your layout is girly, use a font style with curlicues, such as Curlz. If you are creating a school-themed layout, like the one here, you might go for a more "serious" font, like Times New Roman or Arial.

If you have a lot of journaling, emphasize some of the words or phrases in boldface to make them stand out and look more interesting.

Play with color, too. Type your journaling in color instead of black, or highlight certain words or phrases in a different color from the rest of the entry. You can get really creative and type part of your journaling in one font style and part in another!

You Will Need

2 sheets of card stock
in the same color

1 sheet of card stock in
a contrasting color

Letter stickers

tip

Remember, objects look
better off center than
smack-dab in the middle
of the page.

Note that the "School Project" layout uses colors opposite each other on the color wheel. The design looks complicated but is actually easy.

1. Cut the card stock into two 8" × 8" pages.

2. Type your journaling in an interesting manner, using boldface, capitals, punctuation, and different colors, sizes, and fonts.

3. Print your journaling in two parts and cut them out to make two 4¼" × 6¾" blocks that allow space below each for a photo.

4. Crop your photos and adhere them to the journaling blocks.

5. Cut the contrasting-color card stock into two 6" × 7¾" pieces.

6. On the first page, adhere the contrasting-color card stock ¾" from the left edge and ¾" from the bottom.

7. Adhere the first journaling block–photo combo 1¼" from the left edge of the contrasting-color card stock.

8. On the second page, adhere the contrasting-color card stock ¾" from the *right* edge and ¾" from the bottom.

9. Adhere the second journaling block–photo combo ½" from the left edge of the contrasting-color card stock.

10. Apply stickers down the outside borders on the contrasting-color card stock.

Supplies Used: Card stock, Bazzill Basics; stickers, Stickopotamus

I finally got to do the monthly bulletin board. It was **National Book Week**, so I did a **book theme.**

First Ms. Lundquist put blue paper on the bulletin board. I photocopied book covers like **Goose Bumps, Boxcar Children,** and some non-fiction. I glued the covers on construction paper to make them colorful.

I made this really neat sign on the computer. Then I made **GREAT BIG** letters that spelled **R-E-A-D**. I cut them out and stapled them on. Ms. Lundquist said my board was **G-R-E-A-T!**

Today was "Nations of the World" Day. Everybody got a different country. We had to do a report about the customs, language, and other stuff. Then we had to do a project.

My country was **Scotland**. My family is part Scottish so it was interesting to find out about our heritage. Mom had a kilt she let me wear (it was hers when she was a kid). Our next door neighbor let me borrow a plaid scarf and eyeglass case. My teacher said **mine was one of the best reports in the whole class!** I think she liked the Robert Burns poem I put on my poster.

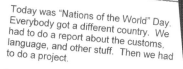

Layout: "Lazy Days"

Lazy Days

Every year I go visit my cousin Matt at Fawn Lake. Matt says a long time ago sharks lived in the lake. We look for shark's teeth on the beach. This year I found four! I beat Matt!

Me and Matt
Fawn Lake

Patterned paper is great for creating shapes or designs. The pages in the "Lazy Days" layout were made from two sheets of patterned paper, trimmed to give the layout a different look.

1. Cut the two pieces of card stock to create two 8" × 8" pages.
2. Crop and mat the photos with the contrasting-color card stock.
3. Cut the striped paper into 3 strips—8" × ½", 8" × 1", and 8" × 1¾".
4. Adhere the ½" strip 2¾" from the left edge of the page.
5. Adhere the 1" strip a little less than ½" from the left edge of the ½" strip.
6. Adhere the 1¾" strip ½" from the left edge of the 1" strip.
7. Adhere the photo 1" from the left edge and 1¼" from the bottom edge of the page.
8. Apply the rub-on transfers or stickers.
9. Adhere the second photo 1" from the left edge and 2½" from the bottom edge of the second page.
10. Cut an 8" × 4½" piece of flowered paper.
11. Use scissors to cut around the flowers from corner to corner. Adhere them to the page, overlapping the photo (it's okay to cover up some of your photograph).
12. Cut a corner from the card stock, and adhere it at the bottom right corner of the page.
13. Apply stickers or rub-on transfers for the title.
14. Make a journaling block, and adhere it to the bottom left of the second page. Apply rub-on transfers.

Supplies Used: Card stock, Bazzill Basics; patterned paper, Pebbles; rub-on transfers, American Crafts

You Will Need
2 sheets of card stock
1 sheet of card stock in a contrasting color
2 sheets of coordinated patterned paper, such as stripes and flowers
Rub-on transfers or stickers

Layout: "It's a Girl Thing"

Have you ever tried using patterned paper as an embellishment? Words, flowers, animals, and other shapes can be snipped from patterned paper to decorate your pages.

The "It's a Girl Thing" layout uses embellishments cut from paper. Plus, this layout has a surprise—a hidden journaling tag!

1. Cut the two sheets of card stock to create two 8" × 8" pages.
2. Crop and mat the photos on contrasting-color card stock.
3. Using your detail scissors, trim a large paper "It's a Girl Thing" flower from the large-flower paper. Adhere it to the right bottom corner of the page. Adhere your photo at an angle over the paper flower.
5. From the small-flower paper, cut two flowers. Adhere them to the page, overlapping the petals on the photo.
6. Cut a piece of small-flower paper into a 7¾" × 7¾" square. Adhere it to the second page.
7. Cut an 8" × 2¾" strip from the matting card stock, and adhere it to the left side of the page.
8. Cut an 8" × 2½" strip from the plaid paper, and adhere it to the card stock border, leaving a ½" edge.
9. Adhere the first photo.
10. Add a thin line of glue around both sides and the bottom of the second photo, close to the edge. Leave the top open to make a pocket.

You Will Need
2 sheets of card stock
1 sheet of card stock in a contrasting color
3 sheets of patterned paper: plaid, large flower, small flower
Corner rounder
Ribbon

tip

Any coordinating paper will work—stripes instead of plaid, ladybugs instead of flowers. An easy way to mix patterns is use papers that come from the same collection.

11. From the card stock scrap, cut a 4" × 2¾" rectangle. Use a corner rounder on top corners.

12. Type or write a journaling block, and then trim it and adhere it to the journal tag.

13. Punch a hole in the top of the tag, and tie the ribbon through it. Slide the tag into the photograph pocket.

Supplies Used: Card stock, Bazzill Basics; patterned paper, Reminisce

When my cousin Lily came to visit, she stayed in my room. We were supposed to be quiet but guess what we really did! Lily will be back next summer. We promised to e-mail every day.

My friend Sofia sent me these pictures from Venice, Italy. Venice has canals instead of roads. People ride in boats everywhere. How cool is that?

Layout: Fall

Stamping is the quickest way to embellish your layout. Stamped images can be colored with watercolor pens, colored pencils, or glitter glue. Stamped images can also be cut out and adhered to your page. The possibilities are endless!

If you've never stamped, practice on scrap paper at first. Rather than stomping the wood block into the pad, rub the pad over the rubber image. Apply even pressure when stamping on paper.

Alphabet stamps are a great way to create titles and journaling. If you want to stamp words neatly, instead of letter by letter, snap a rubber band around a group of alphabet stamps to form the word you want to stamp. If you prefer the casual look of uneven letters and words,

stamp one letter at a time, as shown in the "Fall" layout. Date stamps are a neat way to record the date.

Some stamped images look more natural overlapping each other. Stamp to the edge of the page and even off the page (use scrap paper to protect your work surface). Overlap stamps onto the mats of your photographs. Anything goes with stamping!

1. Cut the two sheets of card stock into two 8" × 8" pages.
2. Crop and mat your photos with the contrasting-color card stock.
3. Cut an 8" × 1½" strip from a scrap of card stock. Adhere the strip to the left edge of the first page.
4. Apply a sticker strip down the center of the border.
5. Adhere the photograph.
6. Stamp leaves on scraps of card stock and cut them out with scissors.
7. Adhere photos to the second page, overlapping corners for interest.
8. Stamp leaf images on both pages. Overlap some images. Stamp other images to the edge of the page.
9. Adhere colored leaves on top of the stamped leaves.
10. Stamp "FALL" with alphabet stamps. Let the letters tumble down the page like leaves.
11. Embellish with stickers.
12. Add date stamp in bottom right corner of second page (optional).

Supplies Used: Card stock, Bazzill Basics; stickers, Bo Bunny; leaf stamp, Rubber Stampede; alphabet stamps, PSX; date stamp, Making Memories; pigment-ink pad, Staz-On

JUMPING *in the* LEAVES

FALL

FALL

OCT 15

Layout: "Who R U?"

Birds and owls have been popular in scrapbooking for some time now. It's a trend that is showing up in clothing, as well.

Scrapbooking supplies such as stamps, patterned papers, chipboard shapes, stickers, and die-cuts sport owl motifs, but you can create your own from scraps of paper by using a template. Add a free-form card stock tree and you have a striking page for your photo. Don't be afraid to draw!

1. Cut the card stock to create an 8" × 8" page.
2. Sketch a tree trunk and two branches on some scrap paper. Leave enough space between the limbs for the owl to perch. Don't bother measuring the tree to fit the page. Adhere tree, then trim ends that are hanging over edges of paper.
3. Trace the owl template onto patterned paper. Cut the body from one pattern, the wings and ears from another.
4. Cut the eyes, beak, and feet from card stock scraps.
5. Glue the owl body to the layout, and add the wings, feet, ears, beak, and eyes.
6. With a pen, outline the owl and add detail. Sketch bark on the tree.
7. Adhere the photo to the page and outline it with black pen.
8. Add title stickers. Add journaling beneath the photo.

Supplies: Card stock, Bazzill Basics and DCWV; patterned paper, MAMBI; stickers, Creating Keepsakes; pen, Sakura

tip

Create your own templates for flowers, houses, and birds. Keep the pieces in envelopes to reuse.

You Will Need
1 sheet of card stock
Patterned paper scraps
Card stock scraps
Alphabet stickers

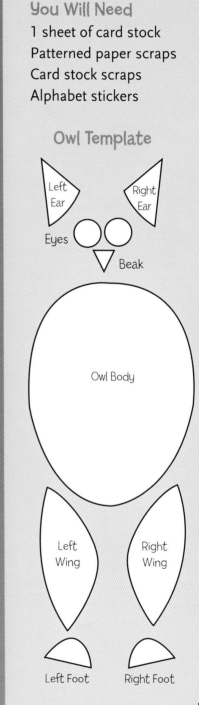

Owl Template

Left Ear

Right Ear

Eyes

Beak

Owl Body

Left Wing

Right Wing

Left Foot

Right Foot

Layout: "Water Butterfly"

Who doesn't love ribbons and bows? Inexpensive ribbons from craft stores add fashion flair to so-so layouts. Ribbons come in narrow, medium, and wide widths. They can be sheer or textured, and they come in luscious colors! You can customize your layout by combining ribbons with other embellishments.

In this layout, "butterfly" ribbons complement the butterfly stickers. Glitter glue hides the staples that attach the ribbons to the page and coordinates with the glittery stickers.

1. Cut 1 sheet of patterned paper to create an 8" × 8" page.
2. Cut a 2" × 8" strip from the second sheet of patterned paper. Adhere the strip to the layout, 1" from the right edge.
3. Mat the photo and adhere it to the page.
4. Apply butterfly stickers.
5. Cut ribbons into 3" lengths. Fold the ribbon pieces in half, and staple them to the layout.
6. Apply rub-on transfers for your title.
7. Cover the staples with glitter glue to make butterfly bodies. Let the glue dry at least six hours or overnight.

Supplies Used: Card stock, Bazzill Basics; patterned papers, Bo Bunny; stickers, EK Success; rub-on transfers, PaperWERX; glitter glue, Ranger; ribbons, craft store

You Will Need
2 sheets of patterned paper
Scrap of card stock
Stickers
Ribbons in several colors
Stapler
Alphabet rub-on transfers
Glitter glue

Layout: "Cute as a Button"

Raid your mother's button jar to create a photo frame that's different and colorful. A lot of scrapbookers simply adhere "naked" buttons to the page. I prefer to "dress" my buttons by tying thread through the holes. The buttons aren't sewn to the page, but they look like they are.

Carry the theme throughout your layout by cutting out by hand a large button journaling block stitched in the center. Scatter more buttons around the title and finish with pen stitching.

1. Cut the card stock to create an 8" × 8" page.
2. Adhere your photo to the lower left corner of the layout.
3. Thread the needle with three to six strands of embroidery floss, depending on the size of the buttonholes.
4. Pull the floss through the buttonholes, and tie it at the back. Trim the ends with scissors.
5. With glue dots, adhere the buttons around the edge of your photo.
6. Using a jar lid, trace a circle on the card stock scrap, measuring approximately 2½" in diameter.
7. Draw four holes in the center of the circle. Thread the needle with more embroidery floss, and sew an X design on the circle. Tie the ends in the back.
8. With your pen, "stitch" around the edge of the paper button. Add journaling.
9. With foam pop dots, adhere the paper button next to your photo.
10. Write your title with alphabet stickers.
11. Thread and adhere buttons around the title. Fill in the "O" with a button.
12. With your pen, "stitch" a broken line connecting the paper button, the title, and the scattered buttons.

You Will Need
1 sheet of card stock
Scrap of card stock
Large needle
Embroidery floss in a variety of colors
Buttons in a variety of colors
Glue dots
Foam pop dots
Alphabet stickers

Supplies Used: Card stock, Bazzill Basics; stickers, Reminisce; embroidery floss, DMC; buttons, craft store

Layout: "Watch Me Climb!"

Felt in scrapbooking? You bet! Felt adds texture and dimension to your layouts and is one of the hottest trends in scrapbooking.

Felt is inexpensive and easily found in craft and hobby stores. You may already have a stash of felt from other projects. Dig out that stash and get ready to make a "fuzzy" layout.

Using your photo as a guide, decide what felt shapes would look best on your page. In the "Watch Me Climb!" layout shown here, felt "boulders" echo the rock-climbing photograph. A hand-cut arrow puts the focus on your photo.

1. Cut the card stock to create an 8" × 8" page.
2. Adhere your photo to the page in the upper right corner.
3. Decide what shapes you want on your page. Hearts, circles, flowers, even dinosaurs are easily cut from felt. Make a paper pattern first, if you want.
4. Arrange felt shapes in the bottom left corner of the layout. Adhere them with small dabs of glue—not too much, or the glue will leak through.
5. Using stickers or rub-on transfers, add journaling in the upper left corner.
6. Hand cut an arrow from card stock scrap. Adhere the arrow so that it is pointing to your photograph.

Supplies: Card stock, Bazzill Basics and DCWV; rub-on transfers, Karen Foster; felt, craft store.

You Will Need
1 sheet of card stock
Felt scraps in several colors
Stickers or rub-on transfers

tip

Make your journaling part of the page. In this layout, the word "CLIMB" runs down the side of the photograph, imitating the action.

Layout: "The Artist"

Sometimes you can't find just the right color for your photo mat—or none of your stickers or embellishments add anything to your theme.

Create an artistic layout using paint samples from the hardware store as your photo mat. There are endless colors to choose from, and simple embellishments are easy to sketch and cut out.

1. Cut the card stock to create an 8" × 8" page.
2. Crop your photo.
3. Adhere the paint strips to the card stock.
4. Adhere your photo on the paint strips.
5. On the unlined white paper, sketch a simple shape, such as a pencil. Cut out your drawing and color it with colored pencils or markers. Adhere the colored drawing to your layout.
6. Write your title on the cutout.
7. Add journaling around the edges of the paint strips.

Supplies: Card stock, Bazzill Basics; pen, Sakura; paint strips, hardware store

You Will Need
1 sheet of card stock
2 paint sample strips
   that coordinate with
   your photo
Unlined white paper
Colored pencils or markers

tip

Some paint names are creative and interesting; let them show as extra journaling on your layout.

Layout: "The Star"

Do you have a special photograph that you want to be the star of your layout? Patterned papers, stickers, and other embellishments may compete with your snapshot.

Put away the patterned papers and get out your scissors and black pen. Add card stock scraps and colored pencils and you are ready to create a "clouds and stars" photo frame like the one shown in "The Star" layout.

1. Cut 1 sheet of card stock to create an 8" × 8" page.
2. Cut the second sheet of card stock into a 7½" × 7½" square. Adhere it to the 8" × 8" page.
3. Mat your photo with a piece of scrap card stock.
4. Center the matted photo on a piece of white card stock and adhere. With a pencil, lightly sketch scallops on the white card stock. Cut out this "cloud" frame and adhere it to your layout.
5. With a pencil, draw several five-pointed stars in different sizes on the other card stock scraps. Cut them out and adhere them to the lower right corner of the cloud frame.
6. With a pen, outline the photo and photo mat.
7. With a pen, outline the white scallops. Repeat the scalloped shape with a pen, adding tiny lines in the cloud edge between the scalloped lines.
8. With a pen, draw tiny five-pointed stars around the layout.
9. Color the cloud edge and the tiny stars with colored pencils. Add a title.

Supplies Used: Card stock, Bazzill Basics and DCWV; pen, Sakura; colored pencils, Prismacolor

You Will Need
2 sheets of card stock
Scraps of card stock in white and 3 other colors
Colored pencils

Layout: "Best Friends"

If you liked doodling in the previous project, you will love this one! Show off your most creative self in this layout that combines doodling, pen stitching, and hand-cut embellishments.

The color scheme in the "Best Friends" layout, shown here, uses both complementary colors (red and turquoise) and analogous colors (red and pink). A black background and the white doodled strip make any photo a standout. This color combination also works great with black-and-white photos.

1. Cut the black card stock to create an 8" × 8" page.

2. Cut the pink card stock scrap into a 5" × 7½" rectangle.

3. Trim one edge of the pink card stock rectangle with decorative scissors. Adhere it to the left side of page, ½" from the top and ½" from the left edge.

4. Cut the scrap of white card stock into a 2½" × 7½" strip. Trim one end with decorative scissors.

5. Adhere the white strip over the bottom part of the pink piece, matching up the decorative edges.

6. Doodle! Draw hearts, arrows, swirls, curlicues, words, birdies, and borders of dots, circles, hearts, and stars on the white card stock strip. Choose one color on your layout (red is used here) and color in a few designs with colored pencils or markers.

7. Cut the scrap of turquoise card stock into a ¾" × 7" strip. Adhere the strip to the far right edge of page, overlapping the white piece a little.

8. Sketch a heart on the red card stock piece, approximately 5" × 6", and cut it out.

9. Adhere the heart over the layout at a slight angle, overlapping the pink, turquoise, and white pieces.

10. Pen stitch around the outside of the red heart.

11. Mat your photo in white. Adhere it 1½" from the top and ¼" from the right edge of the page.

12. Draw a heart on the turquoise card stock, and write your title on it. Adhere the turquoise heart at an angle on the top left part of the red heart, slightly overlapping the pink background.

Supplies Used: Card stock, Bazzill Basics; markers, Sharpie; pen, Sakura

You Will Need
1 sheet of black card stock
Scraps of pink, red, turquoise, and white card stock
Decorative scissors
Markers

Layout: "Cooper"

What a face!
Love my baby!
afternoon in the park

COOPER

Put your punches to work to create a jaw-dropping layout. Frame your extra-special photo in a flurry of hearts and flowers that seem to fly off the page.

This layout is a bit time-consuming, but it's worth the effort. Use up card stock scraps and don't worry about matching colors to the photo. Bright colors stand out against a plain background. The best adhesive for this layout is a glue stick.

Use up "orphaned" alphabet rub-on transfers or sticker letters. Write your journaling in your fanciest style to give your handcrafted layout more artistic flair.

If you hate your handwriting, create a style of printing or a combination of printing and script. Practice a few times, and soon you will have developed your own handwriting "font."

1. Cut the tan card stock to create an 8" × 8" page.
2. Punch a variety of shapes from five or six colors of card stock scraps.
3. Starting in the lower left corner of the page, begin adhering the punched shapes, alternating sizes and colors. As you work, overlap some shapes. Create a diagonal design, ending at the upper right corner of the page.
4. Adhere your photo 1½" from the bottom and 1½" from the right edge of the page.
5. With your pen, draw a thin line around the photo to create a black "mat." Draw scallops around the photo, adding dots in the centers of the scallops.
6. Write your journaling in the upper left corner. Add your title in the lower right corner.

Supplies Used: Card stock, Bazzill Basics and DCWV; pen, Sakura

You Will Need
1 sheet of tan card stock
Card stock scraps
Punches in different
   shapes and sizes

tip

Instead of hearts and flowers, you can use other combinations—try flowers and stars, stars and moons, or snowflakes and flowers.

Layout: "My Birthday Party"

Did you ever play with sewing cards, where you outlined simple designs with yarn? Stitching on paper is very similar. As scrapbooking moves toward a more handcrafted look, scrapbookers are sewing on their pages. Some use sewing machines, but many prefer to sew with embroidery needle and floss.

To create the flower garden effect used in the "My Birthday Party" layout, you will use an easy embroidery stitch called the backstitch. The diagram in step 8 shows you how.

Add punched shapes, hand-cut shapes, and doodling, and you will have a fun, colorful layout.

1. Cut the card stock to create an 8" × 8" page.
2. Punch faces from your photographs using a circle punch.
3. Using card stock scraps, punch three large flower shapes.
4. Adhere the photos to the flowers. Position the flowers on the page, but do not adhere them.
5. With a pencil, lightly sketch flower stems on the page. Draw leaves on green card stock scrap, cut them out, and adhere them to the stems.
6. With an embroidery needle, punch holes in the layout every ¼" or so. These are your stitching holes.
7. Thread the embroidery needle with 3 strands of embroidery floss, and tie a knot at the end.
8. Pull the needle up through the back of your layout, starting at the bottom of your first flower stem. Push the needle through the next hole. The needle will be on the back side of the layout again. Bring the needle up through the third hole, then down through the second hole again. You will have made two stitches. Continue to outline the stems and leaves. Rethread the needle as necessary.
   Stitches on the front of the paper will look like this:

   A   B   C   D   E   F

9. Cut out a half circle from card stock scrap. Adhere it to the upper right corner of your page to create a sun, and trim away the excess. Write your journaling in the sun.
10. With pencil and ruler, lightly sketch "rays" for the sun. With a pen, write additional journaling on the rays.
11. Erase the pencil marks.
12. Adhere the flowers to the stems. Add your journaling or photo captions along the stems. Doodle around the flower petals.

You Will Need
1 sheet of card stock
Card stock scraps
Paper punches
   (circle, flower)
Embroidery needle
Green 6-strand embroidery
   floss

Supplies Used: Card stock, Bazzill Basics and DCWV; embroidery floss, DMC; pen, Sakura

Layout: "House and Flowers"

Now that you have mastered the rules of scrapbooking, try breaking them! More scrapbookers are climbing out of the box of photo matting, color coordinating, and matchy-matchy embellishments to create fun, offbeat pages.

Does this layout remind you of something you did in kindergarten? Good—it's supposed to!

One of the best features of scrapbooking is that you can take it in any direction you choose. You may decide to do more formal, fancy layouts with lots of glitter and rhinestones. Or you may try a funky, casual look. Titles, journaling, even photos are optional.

There are no directions to re-create the "House and Flowers" layout. Use scraps of felt, fabric, ribbons, patterned paper, and pages from magazines—whatever is at hand.

The stitches are meant to look uneven. The doodling is free-form, as doodling should be. The entire layout is pasted crookedly on a larger sheet of card stock. *Wait!* you may be thinking. *This page won't fit in an 8" × 8" album!*

Exactly. The next step in freestyle scrapbooking is to get your pages out of the album. Frame your layouts. Adhere one to the cover of your notebook. Hang one on the refrigerator where everyone can enjoy it.

Now, grab some supplies and sit down at the kitchen table. Let your inner artist out to play!

You Will Need
Card stock
Magazines
Buttons
Felt
Fabric scraps
Embroidery floss
Needle
Pen

Beyond Layouts

Fun Projects, Theme Albums, and Mini-Albums

In the beginning, scrapbookers were happy making layouts for their albums. Then they began creating cards, gifts, and mini-albums.

Now you, too, can create wonderful, one-of-a-kind cards and presents for your friends and family. You won't have to worry about buying the wrong size—and no one ever returns a handmade gift.

In another exciting twist, scrapbookers then discovered that they could "alter" household items for their scrapbooking projects. Clipboards, CDs, coin folders, metal boxes—anything that can be covered with paper and decorated is fair game!

Is it still scrapbooking to make a picture frame out of a clipboard? You bet! It's called "scrapbooking off the page." You use the same materials—card stock, patterned paper, embellishments. Material for other crafts, such as acrylic paints and beads, can be combined with traditional scrapbooking supplies.

Scrapbooking off the page is a great adventure! You'll never look at a clipboard or a mint tin the same way again!

Opposite: Find this Lunch Bag Mini Album on pages 100–103!

Backpack Badge Holder Album

Office supply stores are great places to find inexpensive items to make fun and unusual projects. With plastic badge holders and notebook rings you can create a backpack "album" for yourself and a friend. You need only scraps of card stock, stickers or rub-on transfers, and ribbon. Add photos and a little journaling, and then clip the completed album to your backpack.

1. Using the package insert from the badge holders as a template, cut 12 pieces of card stock, 6 in each of two colors.
2. Decorate one of the pieces of card stock with stickers to create the cover of your album.
3. Adhere your photos to one set of colored card stock inserts.
4. Write your journaling on the other set of colored card stock inserts.

5. Slide the cover and one journaling page into the first badge holder.

6. Slide the photograph that matches the journaling into the next badge holder, with another journaling page behind it.

7. Continue to insert photos and journaling blocks until all 6 badge holders are filled. Insert the back cover behind the photo in the last badge holder.

8. Hook one notebook ring into the slots at the tops of the badge holders.

9. Tie ribbons on the notebook ring, and attach the ring to your backpack.

Supplies Used: Card stock, Bazzill Basics; rub-on transfers, stickers, Making Memories; ribbons, craft store; badge holders, notebook rings, office supply store

You Will Need
Scraps of colored card stock
1 package of 12 clear, vertical badge holders (6 for your album, plus 6 for a second album)
1" notebook rings (one for each album)
Stickers or rub-on transfers
Ribbons

Sports Calendar

This calendar is so easy, you'll want to make a batch of them for presents. Change the theme for gifts for your mother, father, best friend, or teacher. Look for calendars in clear plastic covers in dollar and discount stores.

1. Remove the calendar from the plastic sleeve. Using the calendar as a template, trace around it on a piece of solid colored paper. Cut it out and adhere it to the cover of the calendar.

2. Cut a strip from patterned paper so it measures 1½" wide and matches the length of your calendar. Adhere the strip to the front cover, just below the top.

3. Cut a strip from patterned paper so it measures 3½" wide and matches the length of your calendar. Adhere the strip to the back cover, just below the top.

4. Punch a circle from the solid paper and adhere it to the cover. Apply a rub-on transfer.

5. Apply other rub-on transfers to the front cover.

6. With alphabet stickers, spell "Soccer Games" on the front cover.

7. Apply sports embellishments on the front cover.

Supplies Used: Rub-on transfers, Creative Imaginations; alphabet stickers, Provo Craft; 3-D embellishments, Jolee's

You Will Need
Sheet of plain colored paper (not card stock)
Sheet of patterned paper
Calendar in a clear plastic cover
Rub-on transfers
Alphabet stickers
3-D sports embellishments

Clipboard Photo Album

Here's an album you can hang on the wall! Adding a page is as simple as cutting another sheet of card stock.

The "base" of the album is a clipboard from a discount or office supply store. All you need is acrylic paint, patterned paper, scraps of card stock, and a few trims!

1. Pour the paint into the paper plate. Paint the front of the clipboard and let it dry. Craft paint usually dries within an hour.
2. Cut a piece of patterned paper into a 9" × 9" square, and adhere it to the clipboard 1½" from the bottom.
3. Cut a piece of card stock to create a 9" × 2¼" strip. Adhere the strip along the top of the patterned paper to make a border. (It's okay if the two pieces overlap.)

4. Cut a 1" × 9" strip of patterned paper and adhere it to the center of the border.

5. Cut a 5¼" × 3½" rectangle from card stock. Adhere it to the lower right corner of the clipboard.

6. Cut a 3" × 4¾" rectangle from patterned paper, and adhere it to the card stock rectangle.

7. Cut 3 pieces of card stock, each measuring 6" × 7¼". Cut 3 contrasting colors of card stock, each measuring 4¾" × 5¾" (you can also use patterned paper). These will be your photo mats.

8. Add stickers and tie a few ribbons to the clip part of the clipboard.

9. Mount photographs and hang your clipboard from the little tab in the back.

Supplies Used: Card stock, Bazzill Basics; patterned paper, SEI; ribbons, craft paint, craft store; clipboard, office supply store

tips

These albums are so much fun—make two and give one away to a friend!

You Will Need
Patterned paper
Card stock
Acrylic craft paint
Paper plate
Foam brush
Clipboard
Stickers
Ribbons

Trading Cards in Accordion Envelope Album

Kids have been trading sports cards for years. Why not make your own set of unique cards to trade or to keep? These fun cards have photographs on the front and "statistics" on the back, just like real trading cards.

You'll want to make sets of trading cards on all sorts of subjects: your pets, your friends, your family, even your teachers! Your friends might want to get in on the game and have a card swap.

1. Cut the card stock into 4" × 5½" rectangles for as many cards as you want to make.
2. Crop your photos and mat them on coordinating card stock. Adhere your matted photos to the front of the cards from step 1.
3. Figure out the "statistics" (nicknames, favorite foods, favorite activities, favorite movies, and so on) for each photo.

Name: Mulan

Nickname: Fuzzball

Age: 12

Weight: 9 pounds

Favorite Activity:
Eating!

If she could talk, she would say, "Feed me! More! More!"

4. Type the statistics on a computer and print on plain paper. Mat them with the same card stock as their photo, and adhere them to the back of the card.

5. Apply stickers to the cards.

6. To make the accordion album, you'll need an envelope for each trading card.

7. Line up the envelopes vertically, flaps up.

8. Starting with the last envelope, glue the flap to the bottom of the next envelope. (The flap is adhered to the back of the envelope.) Make sure the flap can be folded so the two envelopes form a "tent."

9. Adhere the rest of the envelopes to one another in the same manner. You now have a chain of glued-together envelopes. Fold the envelopes into an accordion.

10. Leave the flap of the top envelope unglued. Cut a 1½" × 5½" strip of card stock and adhere it to the top flap.

11. Punch a circle from card stock. Apply a sticker in the center of the circle and adhere it to the flap border.

12. Cut a 2" × 5½" strip of card stock, and adhere it to the envelope (part of the card stock will be beneath the flap). Apply a sticker to the strip.

13. Insert one card into each envelope. Fold the envelopes into an accordion, and tie it closed with a ribbon.

Supplies Used: Card stock, envelopes, Bazzill Basics; stickers, Karen Foster; alphabet stickers, Provo Craft

You Will Need
4 sheets of card stock
4½" × 5¾" envelopes (one for each trading card)
Stickers
Alphabet stickers
Ribbon

Babysitting Business Folder

Do you babysit? Walk dogs? Water your neighbors' plants when they are on vacation? Whatever your job, you can keep track of business details in this nifty two-pocket folder.

If you don't have a job, you can tailor the folder to your dance class schedule, scouting activities, or any other activity you are involved in. Or just make it because it's pretty! You'll find a use for it, plus these folders make great gifts.

1. Cut one sheet of patterned paper to create an 8½" × 11" rectangle. Adhere it to the front cover of the folder.

2. Cut a second sheet of patterned paper into a 5¼" × 8½" rectangle, and adhere it to the bottom of the piece you just adhered to the front cover. (You can also use paper scraps to get the same collage effect.)

3. Apply title stickers to card stock scraps (if desired), trim the scraps, and adhere them to the cover.

4. Apply coordinating stickers to the cover.

5. For the inside cover, cut two 4¾" × 9" pieces from the third patterned paper and adhere them to the pockets.

6. Apply title stickers to card stock scraps, trim the scraps, and adhere them to the pockets.

7. Apply coordinating stickers to the pockets.

8. Cut the colored card stock to create two 8½" × 11" rectangles that will be inserted in the front and back pockets.

9. Whatever your job, type an information list (such as name, address, phone number that will be filled in later by hand) and print out. Trim and adhere the sheet for information to one sheet of card stock.

10. Cut the fourth patterned paper to create a 10" × 7¾" rectangle. Adhere this rectangle to the second sheet of card stock.

11. Apply title and coordinating stickers to the front and back pocket inserts.

Supplies Used: Card stock, Bazzill Basics; patterned paper, coordinating stickers, Bo Bunny; title stickers, Provo Craft; two-pocket folder, office supply store

You Will Need
4 sheets of patterned paper
2 sheets of colored card stock
Card stock scraps
Two-pocket folder
Coordinating stickers
Alphabet stickers

Photo-Mat Picture Frame

This frame can be made in less than 30 minutes, using scraps of patterned paper. All you need is a good-quality photo-framing mat.

You can place the decorated mat in a picture frame (minus the glass). The photo-mat frame makes a great gift for your best friend, mother, grandmother, or sister.

1. Place the mat upside down on a piece of patterned paper. Measuring from the top of the mat, mark 6" on the paper. This is the patterned piece that will be adhered to the top of the mat.

2. Trace around the mat, including the opening. Cut this patterned piece out and glue it onto the mat. The paper should cover more than half of the mat.

3. Place the mat upside down on a second piece of patterned paper. Measuring from the bottom of the mat, mark 4½" on the paper. This is the patterned piece that will cover the bottom section of your mat.

4. Trace around the mat, including the opening. Cut this piece out and glue it onto the mat. Don't worry if the two halves don't meet or overlap.

5. Using solid-colored card stock (the patterned paper used in this project reversed to a solid color), cut a 1¼" strip. Cut the strip into two pieces, measuring from the edge of the mat to the opening where the photo is inserted. Place the bottoms of the strips 3½" from the bottom of the mat. Adjust the measurements if your mat is larger.

6. Glue chipboard flowers overlapping the right strip. Place stickers in the top left-hand corner of the mat. Add the stick-on jewel in the center of the biggest flower.

Supplies Used: Patterned paper, Cactus Pink; stickers, Sandylion; chipboard flowers, Prima; stick-on jewel, Making Memories

You Will Need
Pieces of papers in coordinating patterns
8" × 10" photo mat (museum quality has a wider border)
Stickers
3 chipboard flowers
Stick-on jewel

tip

If you can't find chipboard flowers, use stickers.

CD Folder and Card

Ever wondered what to do with all those CD advertising disks that come in the mail? How about those half sheets of patterned papers filling your scrap box? Turn them into greeting cards!

With scraps of paper and a few stickers, you can make a unique CD card in its own special folder. These cards can be created for any special person in your life or for any occasion from your best friend's birthday to Grandparents' Day.

1. To make the envelope, cut the card stock to create a 6" × 12" rectangle. Fold the rectangle in half and crease it.

2. Cut a second piece of card stock into a 6" × 2¾" strip and set aside.

3. Cut scraps of patterned paper into five strips. Adhere them to the front of the CD envelope and trim any excess. Add stickers or rub-on transfers.

4. For the inside of the envelope, cut a scrap of patterned paper into a 6" × 6" square. Adhere the square to the right side of the envelope.

5. Apply glue to the edges of three sides of the small card stock piece (from step 2). Adhere it to the right side of the envelope, creating a pocket. Embellish the pocket with stickers or rub-on transfers.

6. Cut shapes from scraps of patterned paper and adhere them to the left side of the folder. Add stickers or rub-on transfers, if you wish.

7. Trace the CD disk twice on patterned paper. Adhere one circle to each side of the CD, and trim the excess with scissors.

8. Using a jar lid, trace your photo, cut it out, and adhere it to the center of the CD. Add a handwritten message to the back to complete your "card."

Supplies Used: Card stock, Bazzill Basics; patterned paper, Sandylion; rub-on transfers, Creative Imaginations

You Will Need
1 sheet of card stock
Scraps of patterned paper
Stickers or rub-on transfers
1 CD-ROM

Mint Tin Treasure Box

Did you ever wonder what you could do with those cute little mint tins once the peppermints were gone? Make them into treasure boxes with a surprise inside!

Treasure boxes are a great way to use up scraps of paper and ribbon. Add a few embellishments for a one-of-a-kind gift! The treasure box can hold a gift card or personal chore coupons such as "I Will Wash the Dishes for a Week" and "I Will Walk the Dog for a Week."

1. Place the tin on patterned paper and trace it. Cut out one piece each for the top and bottom of the tin.

2. Adhere the patterned paper to the top and bottom of the tin. Trim any overhang with scissors.

3. Cut a strip of patterned paper ½" wide and long enough to wrap around the bottom half of the tin and adhere.

4. Apply tiny glue dots around the top half of the tin. Adhere the ribbon with the glue dots.

5. Trace around the tin on patterned paper again, to make covers for the inside lid and the inside bottom of the tin. Trim them to fit, and adhere them to the tin.

6. Mat a small picture and adhere it to the inside lid.

7. Adhere a silk flower to the cover of the tin and add a button.

Supplies Used: Patterned paper, flower, button, Doodlebug; ribbon, craft store

You Will Need
Small pieces of
  patterned paper
Hinged tin box
Ribbon, ¼" wide
Silk flower
Button

Christmas Gift Bag Album

Gift bags can be used for more than holding tissue-wrapped presents. This album is a great holiday gift! The pockets and tags inside can hold recipes, gift cards, photographs, and stories about how you and your family celebrate the holidays.

Why not start a tradition with a new gift bag album every year? By changing the papers, you can make this album for birthdays, vacations, or other holidays. Even better, you need only a few supplies to create this one-of-a-kind gift.

1. Cut the top off one gift bag so it measures 7" from the bottom to the top. The handles will be removed and you will be left with a pocket. This is your middle page.

2. For the front cover, cut a piece of card stock into a 7½" × 9½" rectangle. Adhere it to the front of a handled bag. Cut a 4½" × 7½" strip of contrasting-color card stock and adhere it as shown. Cut a piece of patterned paper to measure 3¼" × 7½". Adhere it over the card stock strip. Cut a piece of card stock to measure 3½" × 2½". Adhere it in the lower left corner. Cut a piece of contrasting-color card stock slightly smaller than the previous piece and adhere it to the previous piece. Add a sticker.

3. For the inside cover, cut a patterned paper into a 7½" × 9½" rectangle. Adhere it to the bag. Cut a different patterned paper into a 4½" × 5½" rectangle and adhere it.

4. For the front of the middle page, cut a piece of patterned paper to measure 6½" × 7½", and adhere it to the bag. Cut a 3" × 5" card stock mat. For the back of the middle page, cut a 6½" × 7½" card stock rectangle, and adhere it to. Cut another card stock mat to measure 4½" × 6".

5. For the last page, cut a 7½" × 9½" piece from patterned paper and adhere it to the bag. Cut a 4½" × 6" mat from card stock, and adhere it to the bag.

6. For the back cover, cut a piece of card stock into a 7½" × 9½" rectangle and adhere it to the bag. Cut two strips of card stock measuring 1" × 7½".

7. To make inside tags for the two handled bags, cut a piece of card stock to measure 5½" × 7½". Decorate the front and back with photos and scraps of card stock and patterned paper.

8. To make the inside tag for the middle bag, cut a piece of card stock to measure 4¾" × 7¼". Decorate this piece with photos and scraps of card stock and patterned paper.

9. Mark holes at the bottoms of the bags, and punch. Cut ribbons and thread them through the holes. Tie the ribbons loosely so the album can be opened flat.

10. Tie more ribbons around the gift bag handles. Slide the tags into the pockets.

Supplies Used: Card stock, Bazzill Basics; patterned paper, sticker, Bo Bunny; ribbons, craft store

You Will Need
4 sheets of card stock
  (various colors)
4 sheets of patterned paper
  (various patterns)
3 plain white gift bags,
  8" × 10"
Stickers
Ribbons

Zigzag Mini-Travel Album

Mini-albums are the hottest trend in scrapbooking. Instead of making separate travel pages for your main album, why not create a special album just about that fun trip? Once you've made your first accordion album, you'll want to make special albums for the holidays, your pets, your dance recital, your first horse show—any special event.

Mini-albums don't require a post-bound album or page protectors—just card stock, stickers, a few embellishments, and your imagination! In this project you'll use pop dots, those cool foam adhesive squares.

1. Cut both sheets of the same color card stock in two pieces, to create four 6" × 12" pieces, and fold them both in half, forming 6" × 6" folders.

2. Adhere the first 6" × 6" half of one piece of card stock to the second half of another piece. You are creating a zigzag of 6" × 6" squares. The first and last square of your finished zigzag are your front and back cover.

3. For the front cover, cut a 4¾" × 4¾" square from coordinating card stock, and adhere it to the front.

4. For the tag that will go on top of the square on the cover, cut a 4¾" × 2¾" piece from coordinating card stock. Clip the corners on one end. Punch a hole through the tag and tie ribbons through the hole.

5. Apply sticker letters to the tag for the title.

6. Using pop dots, adhere the tag to the front cover at an angle and apply stickers.

7. Cut part of the sheets of coordinating card stock into 4" strips. Cut the strips into 4" pieces that will be used as mats.

8. Decorate the spreads with journaling and photos. For instance, you can type or print your journaling, and mat it on coordinating card stock. You might mat your journaling again on a second color of card stock and do the same for a sticker that you apply with pop dots, overlapping the journaling mat.

9. Mats can be adhered at an angle or as a diamond shape. You can use bands of 1"-wide strips of coordinating card stock to vary your pages. Crop photos and adhere them on the mats, and embellish with stickers.

10. For the back cover, use a larger photo on a coordinating mat and adhere a special phrase below.

You Will Need
2 sheets of card stock
2 sheets of coordinating card stock (different colors)
Ribbon
Stickers

Supplies Used: Card stock, Bazzill Basics; alphabet stickers, Provo Craft; other stickers, Mrs. Grossman's; ribbon, craft store

Composition Notebook Journal

Turn a plain composition notebook into a fashion statement! Sewing notions and fashion-inspired patterned paper make a great "outfit" for a journal. Scrapbook papers can be found in striped, plaid, floral, polka dot, and argyle patterns—just like in your closet! Using papers from the same collection takes the guesswork out of coordinating colors and designs. Once you cover one journal, you'll want to make a dozen!

1. Place the notebook on the back of one piece of patterned paper. Line the notebook up with two edges of paper (this way you have to cut only two sides).

2. Trace around the notebook, excluding the black binding. (You want your paper flush against the black binding when you adhere it). Cut the paper.

3. Apply glue to the notebook cover—edge to edge and in the center—and adhere the patterned paper. Trim the overhanging edges with scissors.

4. From the second patterned paper, cut a strip 1" wide by the length of your notebook. Adhere the strip flush against the binding.

5. Place the notebook on the back of the third patterned paper. Line the notebook up with two edges of the paper. Trace around the notebook, excluding the black binding. Cut the paper.

6. Apply glue to the back notebook cover, and adhere the paper.

7. From the second patterned paper, cut a strip 1" wide by the length of the notebook. Adhere the strip flush against the binding.

8. From the card stock, cut a piece 2½" wide by the width of the notebook, from the edge of the black binding. Adhere the strip 2" from the bottom of the notebook.

9. Cut a 2" × 2" square from the piece of cardboard. Cover it with the third patterned paper. Apply a sticker monogram.

10. Cut a piece of rickrack the width of your notebook, and adhere it to the center of the card stock strip.

11. Adhere the monogram square 1" from the right edge of the notebook.

12. Pin a charm to the rickrack (optional).

13. From the second patterned paper, cut a piece about ½" smaller than the notebook. Adhere it to the inside front cover.

14. For a pocket, cut a 5" × 6" piece of card stock. Apply a thin line of glue around the sides and bottom of the card stock and adhere to lower area of the inside cover.

15. From the first patterned paper, cut a 1" × 6" strip, and adhere it to the pocket 1" from the top.

16. Apply stickers to spell out "Notes."

Supplies Used: Card stock, Bazzill Basics; patterned paper, safety pin, Making Memories; monogram sticker, Basic Grey; alphabet stickers, Provo Craft; charm, craft store

You Will Need
3 sheets of patterned paper
1 sheet of card stock
1 composition notebook
Small piece of cardboard
Rickrack
Large monogram sticker
Small alphabet stickers
Small safety pin (optional)
Charm (optional)

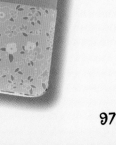

Matching BFF Albums

You and your best friend are tight. You do everything together—share a locker, talk about boys, go to the mall and try on clothes. You nibble pizza, bake brownies, study for math tests—is there anything you don't do together? Why not create special just-alike albums for you and your BFF? These little albums are quick and easy and use few materials. Best of all, there is a pocket in each one to store e-mails, notes, etc. After you work on your matching albums together, your friend may become a scrapbooker, too!

To make two albums, double the materials and do each step twice. First, print a copy of your favorite picture of you and your BFF.

1. Cut two pieces of card stock, each 5" × 7". These are your front and back covers. For the front cover, cut a 2" × 5" strip of patterned paper, and adhere it to the left side of the cover. Cut a design from the patterned paper, and adhere it to the right edge of the strip. Crop and mat your photo, and adhere it over the strip. Add "BFF" in the lower right corner with rub-on transfers or stickers. Leave the back cover blank.

2. From ivory card stock, cut seven pieces, each 4¾" × 6¾". These are your inside pages.

3. Type page headings on your computer: School Pix, Top 5 Songs, Best Movies, Locker Pals, Favorite Books, Boy Survey, Favorite Foods, and so on. Print the headings and cut them into strips.

4. Begin decorating the pages. Cut mats from patterned paper and scraps of card stock and adhere them to the pages. Cut designs from patterned paper or use paper punches to embellish. Keep your pages simple—strips of paper or card stock give the page pizzazz, but remember to leave room for writing and photos.

5. Cut a piece of card stock into a 3" × 6¼" rectangle. Glue the bottom, left, and right sides of the rectangle to the inside of the back cover. This is your note pocket.

6. Stack the covers and inside pages, and punch two holes at the top. Add the notebook rings and tie on colorful ribbons.

Supplies Used: Card stock, Bazzill Basics; patterned paper, Cloud 9; rub-on transfers, Imaginisce; ribbons, Creative Imaginations

You Will Need
Card stock (colored and ivory)
Patterned paper
Scraps of card stock
Stickers or rub-on transfers
2 notebook rings
Ribbons

tip

Punched shapes or stickers can be used in place of patterned paper cutouts.

BOY SURVEY

Best Looking _____

Most Fun _____

Like a brother _____

Rock Star! _____

IMHO

BFF

LOL! SCHOOL PIX

(Yes, that really is us!!)

Lunch Bag Mini-Album

Often you have a handful of photos that represent a special trip or event. Instead of making layouts to add to your 8" × 8" album, showcase these photos in this super-cute album made from lunch bags.

What makes this album special is that photos can be slipped inside the open ends of the bags *and* inside the bottom of the bag. It sounds tricky, but it's really easy. After creating one of these albums, you may never brown-bag your lunch again!

1. Fold each lunch bag in half. Work on each bag separately; to make it easy, we'll call the bags Bag #1, Bag #2, and Bag #3.

2. Cut a piece of patterned paper into a 6" × 6" square. Adhere the square to the front of Bag #1. Add stickers. Open the bag. Cut a piece of card stock into a 6" × 6" square, and adhere it to the left side of the crease.

3. The bottom of the bag should face right. Cut a piece of patterned paper into a 4" × 6" rectangle, and adhere to the bottom of the bag. Cut a piece of card stock into a 4" × 6" rectangle, and adhere it so that right edge "disappears" under the bottom flap. Glue the top and bottom of the flap to create a pocket. Cut a piece of patterned paper into a 6" × 6" square, and adhere it to the back of Bag #1.

4. Cut a piece of patterned paper into a 6" × 6" square, and adhere it to the front of Bag #2. Open the bag. The bottom of the bag should face left. Cut a piece of card stock into a 6" × 6" square, and adhere it to the right side of the crease. Cut a piece of patterned paper into a 4" × 6" rectangle, and adhere it to the bottom of the bag. Cut a piece of card stock into a 4" × 6" rectangle, and adhere it so that the left edge "disappears" under the bottom flap. Glue the top and bottom of the flap to create a pocket. Cut a piece of patterned paper into a 6" × 6" square, and adhere it to the back of Bag #2.

You Will Need
Patterned paper
Card stock
3 brown lunch bags
Ribbons
Stickers

If you run out of certain letters in your sheet of alphabet stickers, an "L" cut into two pieces makes an "I." A "u" turned upside down is an "n." And an "e" can be trimmed into a "c."

When using striped patterned paper, adhere it so the stripes run both from top to bottom and from side to side for added interest.

5. Cut a piece of patterned paper into a 6" × 6" square, and adhere it to the front of Bag #3. Open the bag. The bottom of the bag should face right. Cut a piece of card stock into a 6" × 6" square, and adhere it to the left side of the crease. Cut a piece of patterned paper into a 4" × 6" rectangle, and adhere it to the bottom of the bag. Cut a piece of card stock into a 4" × 6" square, and adhere it so the right edge "disappears" under the bottom flap. Cut a piece of card stock into a 6" × 6" square, and adhere it to the back of Bag #3.

6. For the inside pages, mat your photos and trim them. Punch circles from card stock and adhere them to the back of the photo mat so the semicircle forms a tab.

7. For "hidden pictures," mat the photos and slip them inside the bag pockets.

8. Adhere your photos to the pages, and decorate the pages with stickers.

9. Line up the bags so Bag #1 lies on top of Bag #2, and Bag #2 lies on top of Bag #3. The front of Bag #1 will be the front cover of the album. The back of Bag #3 will be the back cover of the album.

10. Punch three holes through the folds, and tie with three 9" lengths of ribbon.

Supplies Used: Card stock, Bazzill Basics; patterned paper, Bo Bunny and Robin's Nest; stickers, EK Success and Bo Bunny; lunch bags, ribbons, craft store

4

Grand Finale

Throw a Scrapbook Party!

Scrapbookers often get together. They meet in a scrapbook supply store or at each other's houses. While they work on their projects, they talk and laugh and eat. These parties are called "crops."

Why not host your own crop party? Send out invitations to your friends, serve snacks, and share tools and supplies as you work on projects. You could make specially decorated sweet favors and tiny treat boxes filled with hair clips for your guests.

Crop parties often feature a "make-and-take"—a simple project that everyone does together. Before the party, you assemble the pieces. During the party, you instruct your friends on how to make cute hanging CD picture frames.

Preserve the memories of your party. Create a "Scrap Happy" album and have your guests create their own pages. All you do is bind the album. Don't forget your camera!

Tips for Your Crop Party

- ☉ Hold it on a non-school night or a Saturday.
- ☉ Have a theme, such as Pirates, Daisies, or Cats and Dogs. Buy paper plates, cups, and napkins to match the theme. Create a festive centerpiece from items around your house.
- ☉ Serve snacks that won't stain paper or make hands greasy, such as pretzel bites, plain popcorn, candy-coated chocolates, cereal mix, or hard candies.
- ☉ Clear the kitchen or dining room table so everyone has enough space to spread out. In the center of the table, place a basket of scissors, trimmers, staplers, rulers, and other tools that can be shared.
- ☉ Set a candy bar favor, treat box, make-and-take kit, and blank album page at each guest's place.
- ☉ Cropping is hungry work! Serve pizza, sodas, and other messy foods in another room.

You Will Need

Card stock

Scraps of patterned paper

Scraps of card stock

"You're Invited" stamp
   or stickers

Note: All supplies used for the crop party are listed at the end of the "Scrap Happy Album" instructions on page 116.

Invitation

1. Cut a piece of card stock to measure 4" × 5". Cut a piece of scrap card stock to measure 4½" × 3½", and adhere it to the larger piece. Cut a strip of patterned paper, and adhere it to the left edge of the larger piece of card stock.

2. Stamp "You're Invited" on ivory card stock (or use stickers). Color in images if you like. Adhere the stamped card stock to the top of the card.

3. Print the party information on the cards. Make an invitation for each of your party guests, slip the invitations into envelopes, and mail them.

Crop Banner

1. Cut four 5" × 6" triangles from the card stock.

2. Cut a second set of four triangles ½" smaller. Adhere to background. Trim edge of background with decorative scissors.

3. Adhere stickers to spell "CROP." Embellish with cutout designs from paper.

4. Punch a hole at each top corner of triangle. Cut three 7" lengths of ribbon. Thread through holes, except the far left and far right, and tie loosely together. Cut two 15" lengths of ribbon and tie them to the remaining holes. Hang your banner from a doorway or over the table where you'll be scrapbooking.

You Will Need
2 sheets of colored card stock (different colors)
Alphabet stickers
Ribbon

tip

Large alphabet stickers can be found in the teachers' section of office supply stores.

Candy Bar Favor Wrapper

1. Cut a rectangular piece of patterned paper to a width about equal to the length of your candy bar and long enough to overlap when wrapped around the bar.

2. Adhere the paper to the candy bar wrapper. Tie a ribbon around the middle.

Treat Boxes

1. Cut a piece of patterned paper into a 2" × 5" rectangle. Place a matchbox in the center, and wrap it with the paper. Adhere the paper to the matchbox.

2. Trace a matchbox on a scrap of card stock. Cut out the card stock and adhere it to the inside tray of the matchbox.

3. Glue a button on top of the matchbox and fill with tiny treats, such as hairclips or small candies.

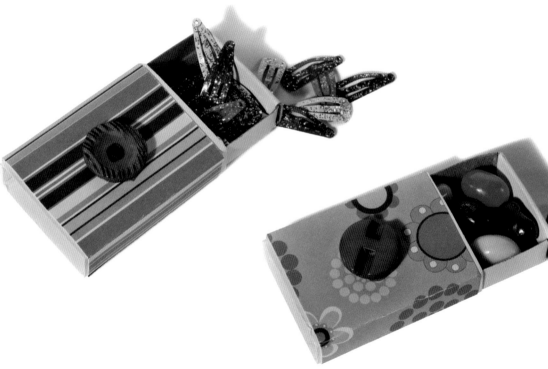

You Will Need
Patterned paper scraps
Card stock scraps
Buttons
Matchboxes
Tiny treats
   (hairclips or candies)

Patterned paper
Card stock scraps
CDs
Ribbons
Stickers
Flower punch

Make-and-Take: CD Hanging Picture Frame

1. Trace the CD twice on patterned paper and cut out the pieces.

2. Cut a 6" length of ribbon. Loop it and, with a dab of glue, hold the ends in place at what will be the top as you adhere the paper pieces to the CD front and back.

3. Trace a round object, about 3½" in diameter. Cut out the circle and edge it with decorative scissors. Adhere it to the CD, slightly offset.

4. Cut a 4½" length of ribbon, and adhere it to the CD at an angle.

5. Punch a flower from the card stock scrap, and adhere it over the ribbon. Add a sticker to the center.

6. This is the sample of the project that you and your friends will use as a guide as you create your make-and-takes. Repeat steps 1 through 6, but don't adhere anything.

7. Place the paper and card stock pieces and CD in a cellophane bag. Using decorative scissors, cut a circle from a paper scrap. Fold the top of the bag, and staple the folded paper over the fold in the bag. Add a snippet of ribbon, if you like.

*Unassembled pieces
for CD Picture Frame*

You Will Need
Colored card stock
Patterned paper scraps
Flower punches

Scrap Happy Album

1. Cut all the card stock into 8" × 8" pieces. Reserving two pieces for the front and back covers, create a page for each guest.

2. For the photo mats, cut card stock into 4¼" × 6¼" rectangles, and adhere them to the bottoms of the pages.

3. For the journaling blocks, cut card stock into 2½" × 3½" rectangles, and adhere them above and to the left side of the photo mats.

4. Punch flowers from patterned paper and card stock scraps. Adhere a big flower to the right of the journaling block. Embellish the journaling block with smaller flowers.

5. At your party, take pictures of each of your guests. If you have a photo printer or computer, print the photos.

6. Let each guest "scrap" her own page by adhering her photo and journaling.

7. With a hole punch, punch holes along the left edge of each page and the covers at 1", 4", and 7". With the back cover on the bottom, stack the album pages, ending with the front cover.

8. Tie ribbons through the holes. Decorate the front cover with a group photo. Add your own journaling on the inside cover, along with a picture of you!

Supplies Used for All Crop Party Projects: Card stock, Bazzill Basics; patterned paper, 3 Bugs in a Rug and Doodlebug; stickers, Stickopatomus; punches, Marvy Uchida and EK Success; ribbon, matchboxes, craft store

Glossary of Scrapbooking Terms

Acid-free—items that do not contain acids that can cause paper to discolor and become brittle and also destroy photographs

Adhere—to mount photos or papers using glue or other adhesive

Adhesive—a substance that glues one thing to another

Analogous colors—colors next to each other on the color wheel

Burnish—to rub (a transfer decal) with a tool for smoothing

Caption—a written description of a photograph

Card stock—heavyweight paper in white and colors, used for base or background of layouts and for matting photographs

Chipboard—thick, stiff cardboard, used for embellishments and covers for handmade books

Complementary colors—colors opposite each other on the color wheel

Composition—the arrangement of pictures and other elements into a specific relation or artistic form

Consumables—items that are used once, such as paper, or used up over a period of time, such as glue and other adhesives

Crop—to cut away unwanted parts of photographs; a gathering where people work on scrapbook projects

Diameter—the length of a straight line through the center of a circle

Double spread—two pages facing each other

Embellishments—accents or accessories used to decorate pages

Freestyle scrapbooking—once you've learned the "rules," taking scrapbooking in any direction you choose

Journaling—a written record of names, dates, and events that can include feelings, stories, and poems; may be handwritten or typed

L bars—flat L-shaped pieces used to create an adjustable frame to decide how to crop a photo

Layout—one page or two facing pages (called a double spread) with one or more photos, patterned paper, decorations, and title; pages in a scrapbook album

Make-and-take—a simple project featured at a crop party that everyone does together and takes home with them

Mat—a border going around a picture or photo

Memento—something that serves as a reminder; a souvenir

Monochromatic—the same color in varying shades, either darker or lighter

Pen stitch—drawing small, sketchy little lines on paper to resemble sewing stitches

Strip journaling—printing a journaling block with space between the sentences, cutting the block into strips, and adhering the strips to the page

Template—a guide (usually plastic) with cutouts used to trace a letter or shape

Acknowledgments and Credits

I would like to thank my agent, Tracey, and my editor, Meredith, both of whom believed I could do this book when I said I couldn't.

Many thanks to Thomas Hopkins Photography, Amanda Miller, Tammie Partanen, Cheryl Reiter, Kathy Smith, and others who provided me with wonderfully inspiring photographs. Special thanks to our talented and energetic models: Ashley, Charles, Cisco, Cooper, Devon, Emily, Hazziza, Jake, Jenna, Kassidy, MacKenzie, Maria, Martha, Matthew, McKenna, Otto, Patricia, Riley, Sarah, Sheila, Simone, Stephanie B., Stephanie W., and Taylor.

I would also like to thank the following suppliers and manufacturers: Bazzill Basics, Autumn Leaves, SEI, Making Memories, Doodlebug, Ranger, KI Memories, Anna Griffin, Me and My Big Ideas, Heidi Swapp, Provo Craft, Polar Bear Press, Sakura, Karen Foster, Reminisce, Pebbles, American Crafts, Design Originals, Bo Bunny, Staz-On, PSX, Rubber Stampede, Stickopotamus, My Mind's Eye, Chatterbox, K & Company, Junkitz, Sassafras Lass, 3 Bugs in a Rug, Jolee's, Creative Imaginations, Die Cuts with a View, Cactus Pink, Sandylion, Prima, Mrs. Grossman's, Basic Grey, Luxe Designs, Scenic Route, Cloud 9, Imaginisce, October Afternoon, PaperWERX, EK Success, Prismacolor, Sharpie, DMC.

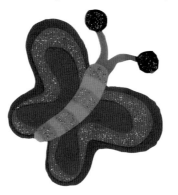

Index

About the Author

CANDICE RANSOM is best known as a writer of award-winning books for young readers (including her popular *Time Spies* chapter book series), but when she's not tapping away at her computer keyboard, Candice can often be found knee-deep in scrapbooking supplies. A mixed-media artist and a former designer for a scrapbook store, Candice has not only made hundreds of projects for herself, but has also taught scrapbooking and journaling classes for people of all ages who wish to preserve their memories in a personal way. Although she writes every day, her creative spirit gets "itchy" if she doesn't take time to immerse herself in patterned papers and embellishments at least once a week. Candice lives in Fredericksburg, Virginia, with her husband, Frank, and their cantankerous cats, Xenia, Winchester, and Persnickety, who modeled graciously for several of the projects in this book.